Spinoza's Ethics

American University Studies

Series V
Philosophy
Vol. 147

PETER LANG
New York • San Francisco • Bern • Baltimore
Frankfurt am Main • Berlin • Wien • Paris

Lewis Schipper

Spinoza's Ethics

The View from Within

PETER LANG
New York • San Francisco • Bern • Baltimore
Frankfurt am Main • Berlin • Wien • Paris

Library of Congress Cataloging-in-Publication Data

Schipper, Lewis.
  Spinoza's ethics: the view from within / Lewis Schipper.
    p. cm. — (American university studies. Series V, Philosophy ;
vol. 147)
  Includes bibliographical references.
  1. Spinoza, Benedictus de, 1632-1677—Ethica. 2. Ethics. I. Title.
II. Series.
B3974.S35   1993   170′.92—dc20   92-37622
ISBN 0-8204-2071-9   CIP
ISSN 0739-6392

Die Deutsche Bibliothek-CIP-Einheitsaufnahme

Schipper, Lewis:
Spinoza's ethics: the view from within/Lewis Schipper.—New York;
Berlin; Bern; Frankfurt/M.; Paris; Wien: Lang, 1993
  (American university studies : Ser. 5, Philosophy ; Vol. 147)
  ISBN 0-8204-2071-9
NE: American university studies/05

The paper in this book meets the guidelines for permanence and
durability of the Committee on Production Guidelines for
Book Longevity of the Council on Library Resources.

Printed in the United States of America.

Dedicated to Teodora, Jenny, Henry, Marcel, the Memory of my Parents, and Miriam

ACKNOWLEDGEMENT

I want to express my foremost thanks, appreciation, and gratitude to Professor Wilhelm S. Wurzer for his valuable advice and helpful comments. I thank Professor Edward Gelblum for his interest in this study. I am grateful to Dr. Heidi Burns and Dr. Robert Ginsberg for their professional counsel and help. I thank Levi Baumohl and Henrietta Yusem for their never failing presence in time of need.

Table of Contents

INTRODUCTION

"I know of no philosopher after Spinoza from whom people can learn as much of significance for our life and community."[1]

This study intends to situate Spinoza's *Ethics* within the context of the person's life. The primary focus is on self- knowledge. It attempts to grasp, comprehend, and integrate the truths of Spinoza's ideas with personal existence. Thus, the reading of Spinoza is personalized.

In general, to personalize knowledge means to reflect on oneself in relation to the subject matter. Thus, the reader and the reading, the reflection and the reflected upon merge into one. It is the most rewarding way to penetrate and comprehend Spinoza's philosophy. It is also the best way to acquire greater insight into ourselves.

"Since reason does not demand anything contrary to Nature, it demands that every one loves himself, looks for what is useful....to attain greater perfection" (EIV, 19, Schol.). To love oneself means to be free to experience life fully and creatively. To be able to do that, we must know ourselves and accept ourselves. This necessitates the clarification of our values, interests, habits, plans, projects, possibilities, etc. It requires insight into the irrational impediments within the self, such as, fears, anxieties, fixations, and all kinds of compulsive behaviors. Self-knowledge involves the whole person in relation to itself, as well as to its environment (family, work, community, political structures, etc.).

In Spinoza's *Ethics* we have a framework in which we can relate the fundamental questions of our existence, involving God, truth and life itself. Everybody needs to answer to these questions. Without them, it is "to lose the reasons for living while trying to live".[2] Spinoza enables us to look at ourselves from the perspective of truth and reason. He teaches us how to discriminate between the important and the unimportant in life. He shows us how to rise above the petty concerns that consume so much of our individual existence. We allow ourselves to become ensnared by what is relatively unimportant in life (our passions), and overlook thereby the things that matter most in life, such as, the knowledge and the understanding of ourselves and of God, both within us and outside us. Spinoza's identification of perfection with reality means that self-elevation is inseparable from self-preservation. Together they constitute human essence.

Whatever we learn from Spinoza is firmly grounded in the reality of life. It can be immediately used and applied to our life regardless of how old or how young we are. Spinoza's Absolute is firmly anchored in the concreteness of our existential being. He answers to our true spiritual needs in a way that is consistent with a fully productive and joyful life. He is a great inspiration to anyone who respects and affirms life, his own and that of others. Spinoza's philosophy is supremely real. He helps us find inner peace and guides us in our way to inner freedom. This is why I read Spinoza lovingly rather than critically.

My aim in this study is to investigate and highlight the aesthetic and existential dimensions of the *Ethics*. The aesthetic dimension pertains to the beauty of Spinoza's text, the elegance of its style, the precision, economy, and richness of exposition, the truth of its content, and the power and wealth of its ideas. The existential dimension deals with the application of Spinoza's thought to problems of existence. These include questions of self-knowledge, self-objectification, and self-awareness as they relate to human potentiality, creativity, and inner freedom. Both areas of inquiry are united in a personalized reading of the text. The study of Spinoza turns into an aesthetic experience when areas of personal existence are illuminated by it. "The more we understand particular things, the more do we understand God" (EV, 24). To appreciate the beauty of Spinoza, it is necessary to read him affectively and thereby grasp his essence intuitively. Spinoza intended the *Ethics* to serve as a guide to the free life. I have endeavored to capture Spinoza's intention in my work, and I have interpreted the *Ethics* in the spirit of its author. Hence, the title: *Spinoza's Ethics: The View From Within*.

"The fact is that Spinoza is difficult...the intuitive or affective reading may be more practical anyway. What if...[one would read Spinoza]...more like the way one attends to poetry? Then difficulty would not prevent the flashes of understanding that we anticipate in the poets we love, difficult though they may be."[3]

My objective in this study is to penetrate into the spirit of Spinoza and interpret the text from the perspective of the whole of the *Ethics*. My aim is to learn from Spinoza and use his deep insights into life in order to better understand myself and know myself. This study is scholarly but not detached. The purpose is to get away from the aridity of conventional scholarship, and unite intellectual rigor with a joyous experience that culminates in true understanding. There will be some room for an element of play and playfulness with the hermeneutics of the text, as discussed by Gadamer. For Gadamer, play is a way to the experience of truth.[4] In Spinoza, the traditional definition of philosophy as the active pursuit of truth together with love of truth achieves its highest expression. Spinoza's concern with truth is unconditional and absolute. It is not tainted with prejudice of any kind. It is totally devoid of personal interest or affect. To understand Spinoza is to understand life. My hope is to have made some contribution to the reading and the understanding of Spinoza.

Notes

1. Arne Naess, "Is Freedom Consistent with Spinoza's Determinism." in *Spinoza, on Knowing and Being and Freedom, Spinoza Symposium,* Assen: Van Gorcum, 1974. p. 6.
2. Gottfried Wilhelm Leibniz, Correspondence Relating To The Metaphysics, Letter XV, in *Discourse on Metaphysics, Correspondence with Arnauld, Monadology,* La Salle, Illinois: Open Court Publishing Company, 1988. p. 171.
3. Gilles Deleuze, *Spinoza: Practical Philosophy,* Translated and prefaced by Robert Hurley, San Francisco: City Lights Books, 1988. p.iii.
4. Hans Georg Gadamer, *Truth and Method.* New York: Crossroad, 1988, pp.91-99.

CHAPTER 1
GOD THE ETERNAL BEING: JAHVE THE ETERNAL PRESENCE

1. Spinoza's God

Spinoza's God has some affinity with JAHWE, the Jewish God, but he is not the God of religion. God is not prior to creation or nature. God is both creator and created, *natura naturans* and *natura naturata*. These, as substance and modes, cannnot be separated. The one cannot exist without simultaneuosly giving rise to the other. The priority of substance over modes is not of sequential successsion. God eternally embraces both. "God is prior to all things by reason of causality" (EI, 17, Sch.). God's causality is nothing but God's activity. As God cannot be separated from activity, so the universe of modes cannot be separated from God's essence. God does not exist without the modes, since they express God's essence. Durational existence of finite modes is connected with God's essence, not with their own. "Whatsoever is, is in God, and without God nothing can be, or be conceived" (E I, 15). While God's essence necessarily involves existence, the "essence of things produced by God does not involve existence"(EI, 24). Modes differ in existence only, not in essence. " Two men may be entirely similar in essence, but must be different in existence" (EI, 17, Sch.).

The relation between nature and its modes is not one of choice but of necessity. The universe could not be other than what it actually is. "From the necessity of the divine nature there must follow infinite beings in infinite ways" (EI, 16). Substance manifests itself and actualizes itself in its modes. The creative and creating aspect of nature *(natura naturans)* is immanent in all things. "God is the indwelling and not the transient cause of all things" (EI, 18). Thus, each finite mode contains within itself some aspect of God's creative powers, *Natura naturans*. God's creative powers inhere in the mode's essence, but their unfolding depend on the mode's existence. Hence, they may or may not actualize themselves. What holds for the (modal) universe as a whole, does not hold for each individual mode. The universe as a whole eternally and necessarily actualizes God's creative powers, but each mode's actualization of its divine creativity depends on its existence.

Modal existence is durational and conditioned. It is conditioned by the mode's own composition, by its necessary connection to other modes, and by its general compatibility with the surroundings. All of these will in various ways affect the unfolding of the divine creative powers within durational existence. Thus, creativity may be promoted, retarded, or even annihilated within the existence of any mode. While each mode expresses *natura naturans* conditionally, the universe of modes (*natura naturata)* expresses it eternally, infinitely, and unconditionally.

The God of Spinoza does not require any proof of existence. Some writers (Wolfson and others) however have argued that Spinoza has used an ontological proof for the existence of God. They claim that the formulation of self caused existence (E I, Def.I), is similar to that used by St. Anselm and later by Descartes. Descartes' idea of a supremely perfect Being must include existence as one of its attributes. Otherwise, the notion of a supremely perfect Being would be contradictory. In the Third Meditation, Descartes says that God is not only the cause of our creation, but of our continued existence.[1] Kant's refutation of the ontological proof is well known. Briefly stated, the refutation is based on the distinction between a logical predicate and a real predicate. The ontological proof is merely a proof from concepts and not from reality. The absence of a contradiction in a concept does not prove its existence in fact.[2] Kierkegaard dismisses the ontological proof by saying that it entails the conclusion as part of the premise.[3]

But all of the above is irrelevant to Spinoza's God. This is so, because God, nature or substance embrace both Being and beings as mutually and eternally expressing each other. Each mode involves Being (the laws of nature) in its existence, and God necessarily involves all beings. Thus, any need to prove God's existence simply does not arise. It is both irrelevant and redundant. The need to prove God's existence goes against the essence of Spinoza's God. A God that is immanent in nature does not require any logical proof for his existence. "Strictly speaking, if God is defined and conceived as Spinoza requires, no proof of his existence is needed." [4]

2. Spinoza's God Is the God of Science

Spinoza's philosophy is compatible with modern science. Consider the astronomer's universe: It consists of billions of galaxies with billions of stars in each galaxy, planets moving around stars, and moons gravitating around planets. All of these movements underlie the same physical laws as those we encounter here on earth. In the vastness of intergalactic space this primordial debris (hydrogen atoms, the most simple atoms of all) is strewn everywhere. The universe is continuously expanding and moving in space. However, no central axis and no privileged location exists in the universe. The universe looks the same regardless of the vantage point from which it is viewed. [5]

The universe is largely empty. Most of the emptiness between the galaxies and the stars approximate an absolute vacuum or perfect void. "There is so much nothing there... that its sum can be substantial".[6] And, "the depth of space may contain at least as many planets like Earth as there are grains of sand on all the beaches of the world." [7]

This majestic vision we get from Spinoza. The greatness of the whole of nature and the radiant view of the universe comes alive in reading Spinoza. We can literally feel how Spinoza's gaze has extended itself into the vastness of infinite space. He called this Infinite, Nature, Substance, or God, (*Deus sive Natura*). The same God, (the ultimate rational principle, the laws of physics and nature), rules the near, the distant, and everything that the mind can conceive of. The whole of reality is governed by the same set of rules. Without them, nothing can be or be conceived.

Spinoza's philosophy must by its nature be consistent with scientific hypotheses and outlook. This is so because *ratio* (reason) underlies both. Spinoza's metaphysics never denies science. It provides the ground for science and thus complements it and extends knowledge into areas that science cannot reach.

3. Spinoza's Metaphysics and the Prevailing Theories of the Origin of the Universe

The two most commonly held theories of the origin of the universe are the Big Bang theory and the continuous creation theory. Most contemporary research inclines toward the Big Bang theory as giving birth to the universe. However, the latest astronomical data put the Big Bang in question.[8] Spinoza's metaphysics is more consistent with the continuous creation theory, although it can also be applied to the Big Bang as the origin of the universe. I will briefly describe, both of these theories to see how Spinoza's metaphysics can be applied to them.

The Big Bang theory holds that space itself had exploded at some primordial instant and that explosion gave birth to the universe. There was no center to the explosion and there was "no primordial clump of matter that suddenly erupted. Space was and is uniformly occupied."[9] All the matter and energy that was ever to be, was there at the moment of birth. Matter and energy will transform into each other for all eternity and their sum will always remain the same.

Fred Hoyle's continuous creation theory,[10] holds that new galaxies are continuously created as older ones recede into the vast expanse that lies beyond the point of all possible observation. New galaxies are being condensed from background material at the rate that the older galaxies recede. At any one time, the number of observed galaxies remains unchanged. The same holds for the background material at large. Such material consists largely of hydrogen atoms. Its average density stays the same. The reason why the background material is not being exhausted throughout the process of galactic condensation is the continuous creation of new material to compensate for the loss of old matter. Hoyle concludes that "the nature of the universe requires continuous creation."[11] Matter in the form of hydrogen atoms is continuously created anew in the universe. To the question, where does the material come from, Hoyle says, that it simply appears, it is created.[12] He hypothesizes that the average rate of formation of new matter amounts to "no more than the creation of one atom in the course of about a year in a volume equal to that of a moderate sized skyscraper."[13] It is quite impossible to detect such creation by experiment. For the entire universe, the creation of new material is extremely large. It provides an outward pressure for the expansion of the universe. The galaxies are continuously expanding into an infinite space. "There is no end to it at all."[14]

4. Reconciliation with Spinoza's Metaphysics

The Big Bang can be seen as an outburst of cosmic energy in the attribute of Extension. Extension is an attribute of God, and is one view of the essence of substance (EI, Def. 4). As such, its power is infinite. The explosion of energy (matter) may be seen as the immediate infinite modification of substance, (i. e. motion and rest) in the attribute of Extension. All matter or energy was formed in an instant of time. After that, energy or matter were only to be redistributed, not created. The ensuing cooling off of matter led to the expansion of the universe, giving rise to *facies totius universi,* as the mediate, infinite modification of substance. This proces of expansion is continuous and ongoing.

In the original explosion of space, energy was released, and matter in the form of hydrogen atoms was created. Finite modes (hydrogen atoms as the simplest elements of matter) evolved from the infinite, immediate, and mediate modification of substance. The modal evolution of the cosmos has since proceeded by necessity from finite (durational) causes. With the birth of the universe, time itself came into being. Thus, "every individual thing, or everything which is finite and has a conditioned existence, cannot exist or be conditioned to act, unless it be conditioned for existence and action by a cause other than itself, which is also finite and has a conditioned existence; and likewise this cause cannot in its turn exist, or be conditioned to act, unless it be conditioned for existence and action by another cause, which also is finite and has a conditioned existence, and so on to infinity" (EI, 28).

The continuous creation hypothesis of the origin and expansion of the universe corresponds to Spinoza's active and passive powers (or principles) of substance, *Natura naturans* and *Natura naturata.* Active and passive substance, or ground and consequent, are an eternal and necessary expression of the same, (Nature, God, or Substance). God expresses his essence through an infinity of attributes. Attributes are the eternally active and infinite manifestations of being of substance. Each attribute expresses the essence of substance. Nature viewed as active is the eternally creating and self-creating substance. It is "that which is in itself and is conceived through itself... God in so far as he is conceived a free cause." God, nature, or substance are one, indivisible, eternally creating, and infinitely active. God's existence and his infinite power and activity are the same. *Natura naturata* or nature viewed as passive is "all that which follows from the necessity of the nature of God.... all the modes of the attributes of God.... which without God cannot exist or be conceived" (EI, 29, Note). *Natura naturata* includes the universe of infinite and finite modifications of substance. Substance and its modifications do not form a sequential order but stand in a logical order of causation. Substance and modes cannot be separated from each other. God eternally embraces and involves both. The relation between nature and its modes are those of ground and consequent. Without the ground there is no consequent. God is the ground of Being *(natura naturans)* and the infinite diversity of beings *(natura naturata)* can neither be nor be conceived without God as their cause. Each mode contains within itself the essence of the whole. God connects all things in nature to his essence. *Natura naturans,* as the eternally active substance is to be viewed *sub species aeternitatis,* under the mode of eternity. Modes have a conditioned existence, and the modal universe may be viewed both through the mode of eternity *("sub species aeternitatis"),* as the immediate and mediate infinite modes of substance, and through the mode of duration, *("sub species durationis")* of the finite modes.

Modern science believes that the universe is *"infinite* in extent and will expand *forever."* [15] And, "if future studies verify these conclusions, the implications are staggering, for who can claim to comprehend infinity and eternity?"[16] I contend that among all the philosophers, the genius of Spinoza truly comprehended infinity and eternity. The continuously expanding universe is Spinoza's *"facies totius universi,"* the face of the entire universe. It is the mediate, infinite, and eternal mode of substance within the attribute of extension. The laws of nature are inscribed in it. The immediate, infinite, and eternal modification of substance within the same attribute is motion and rest. All finite modes are modifications of motion and rest, or physical energy, within the face of the universe. In the universe there is a rational (and logical) progression of causes, both vertically, from substance to mode, and horizontally, from mode to mode. Causes are the same as actions and causality in general signifies activity. God in the infinity of his attributes is self-caused *(causa sui)* and thus eternal. Attributes have a logical priority over the infinite and eternal modes. This is the sense in which the infinite and eternal modes are caused by God and can only be conceived through God. The finite modes find their cause in the immediate and mediate infinite modes. Thus, the whole universe is linked together by a unified system of causes, and "whatever is, is in God and without God nothing can be, or be conceived" (EI, 15).

I have attempted in the above to reconcile Spinoza's metaphysics with contemporary scientific views about the creation of the universe. However, nature as *natura naturans*, the creating principle, and its immediate and mediate infinite modes, (motion and rest and the face of the universe), eternally coexist. Since in eternity there is no before and after, or succession, God as the creating principle can only have a logical priority over the immediate and mediate modes, not a real priority, or a priority in time. Since motion and rest cannot take place in a vacuum, there must have been some kind of matter, (subatomic particles?) to carry motion and rest. The entire cosmic energy may have been compressed in a point, which exploded in the Big Bang and gave rise to the universe. This is compatible with the explanation given by the Kabbalah, the Jewish mysticism, in the book of Zohar.[17] The question raised was, how did the finite evolve from the infinite? And the answer given was through Tsimtsum, which meant, the simultaneous and instantaneous compression and release of the infinite cosmic energy.[18] This is quite similar to the modern Big Bang theory.

5. How Does Spinoza's Metaphysics Relate to Modern Quantum Physics?

In the world of quantum physics, nature is viewed as discrete rather than continuous. Matter is made up of atoms, little particles that move around in perpetual motion. Even light consists of tiny quanta (particles) called photons. This quantum world of subatomic particles is non-objective, non-deterministic and subject to "observer created reality".[19] We cannot think of an electron as an ordinary object located in space and time. We cannot locate an electron in a given space at any time. Subatomic particles behave in random fashion. Electrons jump around the nuclei of the atoms randomly. In this quantum microcosm, particles (electrons) appear as waves, and light waves appear as particles (photons). We cannot determine any specific event by itself. We can only determine the probability distribution of events. That is, an electron's position and momentum can only be determined through its probability distribution. In the subatomic world, the distribution of events, and not the events themselves, is causally determined.

In the world of quantum physics, the prevailing mode is uncertainty. What we see depends on the observer. The outcome of a given experiment depends on the intention of the experimenter. In line with Heisenberg's uncertainty principle, the act of measurement itself influences the result. The very act of observing changes the electron's place. We cannot simultaneously determine the position and the momentum of an electron. If we try to determine one, we cannot know the other. We can only give a statistical description of these events.

Perfect randomness prevails in the quantum world. The complete randomness of individual events assures the stability of their probability distribution. What we have here is not the classical determinism of individual events (these are perfectly random), but the quantum determinism of a collectivity of events. Individual events in the subatomic universe are not subject to physical laws that prevail in the macro-world. This makes the micro-universe indeterminate. If however, behind the quantum world there was still another level of reality (a sub-quantum universe), that determines quantum behavior, the deterministic view of nature would still hold. Einstein never gave up the deterministic view of the universe.

The idea of perfect randomness contains in itself a lawfulness. Such randomness gives rise to stable probability distributions. The perfect arbitrariness of individual events guarantees the absolute lawfulness of their collective behavior. While individual events are indetermined, their collectivity is determined. It is a statistical determination rather than a physical one. A change in the probability distribution will bring about a different projected outcome. For any stable probability distribution, the likelihood of events occurring over a certain time are based on the law of averages and are thus predictable.

The question presents itself now, how we can reconcile the above with Spinoza's metaphysics, where "all things are conditioned to exist and operate in a particular manner by the necessity of the divine nature"(EI,29). The following possibilities present themselves:

(1). Perfect randomness implies lawfulness, just like perfect disorder implies order that is inherent in the idea of perfection. The order inheres in the completeness (or perfection) of the disorder.

(2). Such perfection of disorder brings about a probability distribution that is stable, and whose events are predictable, "chaos can be related to chaos in an ordered way."[20]

(3). If a still deeper level of reality that determines the randomness of the quantum world exists, then the subatomic universe would also be determined.

(4). Events in the physical world are also randomly located within a probability distribution. Given all the factors that bear on air traffic fatalities for a given year, that is, given all the factors that determine the probability distribution of airplane accidents, we could predict with great likelihood the total number of people who will die due to traffic accidents in a given year. But we cannot predict who these people will be. Their fate will be randomly determined. The probability distribution can be altered (we can enforce better safety rules, etc.) which will lower the number of airline fatalities, but the accidents will still be randomly distributed.

All of us operate within the context of given probability distributions of which we are not aware. The odds of events happening to us are determined by such invisible distributions. Since we are not aware of these probabilities, we think of ourselves as being free to determine the course of our life. Such freedom is merely illusory, since it expresses our lack of knowledge of the causes that determine and shape the probability distributions within which each of us is enmeshed. We can enhance our freedom only by an enhanced awareness of our constraints. To the extent that we alter our probability distributions, we alter the probability of desirable or undesirable events occurring. Each of us is located in an almost infinite number of probability distributions, due to heredity and the environment. The impact that we have on altering these distributions is small indeed.

(5). Spinoza's God is not the same God as that of Leibniz or Descartes. The God of Leibniz and of Descartes is transcendent. God determines every event in nature for all time (Leibniz), and at all times (Descartes). The God of Spinoza is immanent in nature. *Deus sive natura* means that whatever nature is, it eternally expresses the divine essence.

6. The Modal Evolution of the Universe

Primordial matter consisted entirely of hydrogen atoms, the simplest, chemical element. In high temperatures (the Big Bang), hydrogen atoms collide and fuse into helium. These elements, hydrogen and helium, dispersed as space cooled and from them the background material for the galaxies was formed. Stars go through a cycle of birth, maturity, and death (lasting billions of years), and in the process, the light atoms are converted into heavier, chemical compounds, such as carbon and other molecules. Carbon molecules formed the base upon which all subsequent life (flora and fauna), was to depend. When the planet Earth cooled and solidified, the engendered steam condensed into oceans.

The first living matter evolved from non-living matter. After that, life gave birth to life, leading to the evolution of all living systems. Conceivably, the emergence of life required the coming together of uniquely suitable conditions that may have happened only once on our planet. From this initial process, life progressed to the emergence of human consciousness.

Evolution consisted in the adaptation and replication of existing species as well as in the formation of new species through mutation and through the occurrence of other causes and conditions. "There is necessarily for each individual existent thing a cause why it should exist" (EI, 8, Sch.). "Bodies are distinguished from one another in respect of motion and rest, quickness and slowness, and not in respect of substance " (EII, AX.II, Lemma I.).

The most simple bodies differ only in motion and rest, or quickness and slowness. The more compound bodies consist of systems of basic bodies with various levels of energy (speed and slowness) that preserve a fixed relation between them. These together compose one body or an individual (EII, 13, Ax 2, Def.). A change in the nature of a given body (an individual) takes place when the given relation between motion and rest in the constituent parts is altered. However, "If the parts composing an individual become greater or less, but in such proportion, that they all preserve the same mutual relations of motion and rest, the individual will still preserve its original nature, and its actuality will not be changed" (EII, 13, Lemma 5). Thus, "a composite individual may be affected in many different ways, and preserve its nature notwithstanding"(EII 13, Lemma 7, Note). We may conceive "the whole of nature as one individual, whose parts, that is, all bodies, vary in infinite ways, without any change in the individual as a whole" (ibid, Note).

All of nature is an interconnected whole. Like an individual, it consists of systems and subsystems, each one depending for its proper functioning on the totality of all. Nature can be compared to the mythical Goddes Gaya, who had all living things as its organs, each organ only functioning with all the others and not by itself. Nature provides everything it needs for its optimum functioning. It provides its own support systems.

It is logical to assume, that within nature the process of creation, recreation, and transformation of systems of motion and rest, (energy systems), leading to system differentiation and new formation never ceases. This process (of *natura naturans* within *natura naturata*) never really stops. It is eternal and infinite. The evolution of matter, the forming of new chemical compounds, the transformation of inorganic into organic structures, the occurrence of simple life cells (unicells), the biological evolution of the species, are all eternal, timeless and continuous processes. All creation is continuous, but not necessarily repetitious. The emergence of life may well have been a unique event in time. This does not exclude the possibility of several such beginnings or that such changes may not come about in the future.

Evolution of consciousness and cultural evolution may also be considered as continuous processes in time. These evolutions, like the rest of nature, do not necessarily proceed smoothly and without shocks. They do build upon themselves and follow the natural pattern of creation in the universe. This takes us directly to the question of human creativity and of human genius. Human genius is largely the case of allowing nature its freedom to unfold, and not subjecting it to the bondage of the human will or desire. People and nature need to be let to function on their own terms, without putting hindrances in their way. Nature's as well as the individual's creative powers, can only fully unfold in freedom from artificial constraints. The primary constraints upon nature are those caused by society through environmental destruction, and the primary constraints upon our creativity are brought about by the inner pressures exerted upon us through our will. Only by the imposition of force through the human will, can the freedom of nature and that of individual be interfered with and inhibited. The results of such interference can only be, in the long run, destructive to both.

7. The Scientific and Extra-Scientific Dimension of Spinoza's Metaphysics

Spinoza's philosophy is scientific because it, like science, deals with nature itself. By placing God in nature, it left behind all purely idealistic, religious, and unscientific pathways that search for the supernatural. Nature's creative forces were seen to be the same everywhere, but expressing themselves differently. It inspired Einstein's search for a "unified field theory," a theory which would unite in one equation or intuition all forces operating in nature, such as, electromagnetic and gravitational forces, strong and weak subatomic forces. Einstein was not able to solve this problem, but scientists have not given up on the project of finding a way to unlock all the secrets of the universe.

Science however is not philosophy, and physics is not metaphysics. Science can only analyze what is accesible to it. Such access need not be restricted to the senses, even when enhanced through the most poweful instruments available to us. No matter how powerful the instruments may be that we can design, they will always remain an extension of sense perception and of our analytical judgment. Science will always remain on the level of analysis, and scientific intuition must ultimately be subject to perceptual verification if it is to remain within the paradigm of science. Science can only deal with parts of reality. It can never encompass the whole of reality.

That is why metaphysics is necessary. Metaphysics seeks the understanding and the knowledge of the whole, a whole which science can never attain. Einstein's preoccupation over half of his life with "a unified field theory" was a scientific search for the key that would unlock the universe from within. The knowledge of the whole of nature or God cannot be achieved through science. Even the greatest achievements of science, can only be made within the context of segments of reality. They cannot pertain to reality as a whole. The latter must be left to the metaphysicians. Spinoza's metaphysical intuition of *natura naturans* acting upon *natura naturata* most probably inspired Einstein in his search for the ultimate answer to all of nature's riddles. We cannot discover *natura naturans* through the tools of science. Only metaphysical intuition can lead to its unraveling. Metaphysics seeks to reveal what science cannot. Science cannot place itself inside the thing that it tries to understand. Science can only approach the thing from the outside. It cannot grasp the thing in its actual flow of being. In order to perceive, catch and analyze the flow, it must necesarily break it. Metaphysics, on the other hand, is able to place itself inside the thing. It can catch the very flow of being (movement and life) within the thing. The metaphysician can grasp reality in its uninterrupted and undivided totality. To the extent that science and metaphysics seek to understand the same reality, to this extent they enhance and complement each other. While Spinoza's metaphysics is scientific in its quest for truth, it can never be reduced to mere science. Spinoza's philosophy penetrates into nature itself and intuits God within it. It thereby opens possibilities for science to guide it into the path of nature and God. It exerted a powerful stimulus to science, and it inspired eminent scientists in their search for knowledge. When Einstein was asked whether he believed in God, he answered: "I believe in Spinoza's God who reveals himself in the orderly harmony of what exists, not in a God who concerns himself with the fates and actions of human beings."[21]

Notes

1.   Rene Descartes, *Meditations on First Philosophy*, in *The Philosophical Works of Descartes*, Translated by Haldane and Ross, Cambridge: Cambridge University Press, 1970. vol.I, pp.157-171.
2.   Immanuel Kant, *Critique of Pure Reason*, Transl. by F. Max Muller, New York: Macmillan Co. Anchor Books Edition, 1966, pp.404-413.
3.   Soren Kierkegaard, *Concluding Unscientific Postscript*, Transl. by David F. Swenson and Walter Lowrie, Princeton: Princeton University Press, 1974, p.298.
4.   Errol E. Harris, *Salvation From Despair*, The Hague: Martinus Nijhoff, 1973, p.39.
5.   Subhash Kak, *The Nature of Physical Reality*, New York: Peter Lang Publishing, Inc. 1986, pp.59-60.
6.   George A. Seielstad, *Cosmic Ecology: The View From the Outside In*. Berkeley: University of California Press, 1983. p. 6.
7.   Ibid., p.4.
8.   See, "New data on Galaxies Jolt Vital Element of Big Bang Theory", New York Times, January 3, 1991.
9.   Seielstad, p. 45.

18

10. Fred Hoyle, *The Nature of the Universe.* New York: The New American Library, Harper & Brothers 1955.
11. Ibid., p. 111.
12. Ibid., p. 112.
13. Ibid., p. 114.
14. Ibid., p. 115.
15. Seielstad, p. 49.
16. Ibid., p.49.
17. Zohar The Book of Splendor, Basic Readings in the Kabbalah, edited by Gerschom G. Scholem, New York: Schoken Books, 1972, p.27.
18 . In the Lurianic doctrine of the Kabbalah, "the first act of the Ein Sof [the Infinite] was not one of revelation and emanation but on the contrary, one of concealment and limitation." Tsimtsum signifies "the entry of God into Himself." *Encyclopedia Judaica,* vol.10, New York: The Macmillan Company, Jerusalem: Keter Publishing House, Ltd., 1971, p.589.
19. Heinz R. Pagels,*The Cosmic Code.* Bantam Books, 1984. p.47.
20. Ibid., p. 96.
21. Cited in, Hans Kung, *Does God Exist? An Answer for Today.* New York: Vintage Books, A Division of Random House, 1981.p. 62.

CHAPTER 2
THE MIND BODY PROBLEM:
CONSCIOUSNESS AND SELF-CONSCIOUSNESS

1. The Psycho-Physical Parallelism

To fully appreciate Spinoza's mind-body parallelism, we must start with his definition of an idea. An idea is a modification within the attribute of thought, exactly the same way as a body (thing) is a modification within the attribute of extension. Given the absolute equivalence of all of God's attributes, each one expressing the infinite and eternal essence of substance, any one modification will of necessity be subsumed equally under any of God's attributes. Since the human mind can only conceive two of God's infinite attributes, namely, the attributes of thought and extension, there will of necessity be a perfect correspondence of any mode with regard to these two attributes. Thus, "The order and connection of ideas is the same as the order and connection of things" (EII, 7).

The infinity of God's attributes follows directly from the infinite power of God. The human mind can conceive only the attributes of thought and extension because we consist of these. However, to restrict God's power to only two of the attributes accessible to the human mind, would be a negation of God's essence (since "all determination is negation".) An attribute is defined as "that which the intellect perceives as constituting the essence of substance" (EII, Def.4). An infinite intellect or understanding, is the immediate, infinite mode in the realm of thought. The human mind is a modificaton of substance in the attribute of thought. This immediately raises the Tshirnhaus problem (expressed in letter 65) of whether the attribute of thought has a privileged position with respect to all of the other attributes. This would be so, since the idea must accompany each mode in all of the attributes, as well as retain its own ontological status of an equivalent mode in the attribute of thought. The problem is resolved through Def.4 (the definition of an attribute). The infinite intellect or understanding is an absolute power of God (same as the power of existence). This understanding, (itself a modification within the realm of thought) pertains to the equivalence of the idea (thought modification) and its object (under any of the infinite attributes). The parallelism between an idea and its object is an epistemological one. The object (a mode of substance) occurring under any and each of the infinite attributes will be conceived through the infinite power of comprehension (the correspondence of the idea and its object), but it will also retain its ontological equivalence (the identity of the given mode under all the attributes). What we have here is an ontological parallelism between a given mode under different attributes, and an epistemological parallelism between the idea and its object. Each attribute eternally expresses God's essence through the same mode. The ontological parallelism between mode and attribute expresses God's infinite power of existence. Surely, the infinite powers of existence and comprehension must relate to all of God's attributes and modes. Existence and comprehension are not attributes but expressions of God's infinite powers, which pertain to God in God's absoluteness (totality).

This takes care of the Tshirnhaus' problem. Neither of the attributes has a privileged position relative to any other. Thought as an attribute is not ontologically privileged. It is not the first among equals. However, in an epistemological sense, (in terms of God's infinite understanding), a modification of thought (idea) must accompany any of the other attributes and all of their modes. Thus, any one of God's attributes can only be conceived through a modification within the attribute of thought, and "every idea is in God...."(EII, 3).The similarity of God's power of Understanding (infinite intellect) and God's power of Being (absolute existence) is self-evident. They both express the eternal and infinite power of God. The power of existence *(onto, esse)* and the power of comprehension *(episteme)* accompany all of God's attributes (the infinite ways of expression of God's essence). Existence is not confined to the attribute of extension, but it accompanies all of them. Similarly, understanding is not confined to the attribute of thought, but it accompanies the conception of an idea (a modification in the realm of thought), with respect to its *ideatum* (object) in any of the infinite attributes. God's infinite attributes necessarily include the attribute of thought as well (the idea of an idea).

Spinoza's mind and body do not represent a unified mind- body set. One is not indistinguishable from the other. To the contrary, mind and body are distinct from each other. In this sense, Spinoza follows Descartes and he does not depart from the philosophical tradition. However, Spinoza changes the context of mind and body. They are not independent substances, as in Descartes. Mind and body are parallel expressions of the same substance, which is the cause of both. Mind and body are united in their cause. The Cartesian split of mind and body and the resulting dualism of two substances absolutely independent of each other ("my soul...is entirely and absolutely distinct from my body and can exist without it"),[1] has been resolved into one substance (God or nature), underlying both.

The main philosophical tradition, from Plato through the medievals, such as St. Augustine, and up to Descartes, had denigrated nature relative to Spirit. (For Hegel, nature is alienated Spirit.) Spinoza put God back into nature, spiritualizing thereby both nature and the human body.This had its beginning in Democritus, Epicurus, and the Stoics.

The human mind, says Spinoza, is nothing but its ideas. The mind perceives ideas of the body and any of its affections. Ideas have their exact counterpart in things. Thus, "the first element which constitutes the actual being of the human mind, is the idea of some particular thing actually existing" (EII, 11). Modifications in the realm of thought and in the realm of extension are exactly parallel to each other (EII, 7). This parallelism implies independence, but not separation. Body and mind as equivalent modifications of God's essence in the realm of thought and in the realm of extension are independent of each other, yet they are bound together by necessity. The correspondence between them is absolute. There is nothing in the world that would or could take place in the one without simultaneously taking place in the other. Whatever takes place in the body (all possible affections, *"affectiones"*) will always have their exact counterpart in the mind.

Spinoza's mind is not a collection of ideas. It is not an independent or separate receptacle which can be filled or emptied of ideas. The mind in itself does not exist. Only ideas exist. Therefore, we cannot concretely speak of a mind separate from its ideas or thought modifications. The human mind does not exist apart from the ideas that it expresses. For Descartes, thoughts and ideas are properties of the mind (an independent substance). For Spinoza, there is no mind that possesses any number of properties. There are only ideas which we call the human mind.

2. Degrees of Animation

Since there is no mind in itself, only ideas or thought modifications, what we normally refer to as mind is not restricted to human beings. All ideas take their origin in God (nature or substance). This is equally true of a grain of sand, a worm, an airplane or a part of human skin. What we call life is the mental counterpart of things. The mental counterpart of a grain of sand or a bar of iron, is its idea that is in God. Such ideas represent the most simple level of the spiritual realm. As we advance from the inorganic (so called inanimate) to the organic (and animate), from the most simple to the most complex, the degree of animation is compounded at each step of the way. Every part of a more complex individual is alive by itself as well as by its being a part of a living organism. To the extent that we share in God's ideas, whether actively or passively, by perception or conception, only to this extent do we comprehend ourselves and nature. Through comprehension and understanding, we partake in nature's essence. Our comprehension, understanding, and intellect are part of God's infinite understanding. The infinite intellect, as an immediate and infinite modification of substance in the realm of thought, is parallel to motion and rest, as an immediate and infinite modification of substance in the realm of extension. On the level of body, we partake in motion and rest. On the level of mind, we partake in the infinite intellect. All ideas, however, are in God, irrespective of our knowledge or comprehension of them. Since each thing in the realm of extension has its correlate in the realm of thought, and since we refer to such correlates as mind or mental, an idea exists (in God) of each body regardlesss of its composition, whether simple or complex. Hence, all of God's universe is animated (EII, 13, Note). Bodies differ in degrees of motion and rest, quickness or slowness, etc. This emphasizes the unity of nature in its most fundamental aspect, the form of its elemental force or energy levels. We are accustomed to restrict the notion of life only to those forms of nature which exhibit motion, sensitivity, and soul. But, according to Spinoza, the restriction is merely conventional. It is too limited. Elemental energy forces belong to the entire range of the extended universe and to their counterparts in the realm of thought or the realm of life. The realm of life encompasses the infinite intellect with all its modifications in the form of the mental (ideas). Moreover, all bodies have sensitivity to the extent that they can affect and be affected by other bodies. On the level of the most elementary particles, the microcosm, atoms collide, form molecular chains, and so on. They act and interact through complex processes, all of which have their precise counterpart on the level of thought and animation. They affect and are affected by each other through levels and intensities of motion and rest, elemental energy levels. Thus, the conventional division within the realm of extension into the animate and the inanimate, live and dead matter, is not absolute. Differences in degree of animation occur, differences in levels and complexities of bodies. These range from the most simple bodies to the most compound individuals consisting of many sytems and subsystems. Ultimately, nature itself can be viewed as an individual consisting of many systems of parts, each connected with every other. Whatever happens to any one part will affect all the other parts. Thus in nature is a continuous composition and decomposition of matter, life turning to death, and death turning to life, an ongoing cycle of change and transformation, eternally expressing God's essence as *natura naturans* and *natura naturata*.

3. Individual Modal Differences

Bodies differ with respect to motion and rest, quickness and slowness, but not with respect to substance (EII, 13, Ax.II, Lem.I). Bodies also differ with respect to their ability to perform actions and receive simultaneous impressions. These powers of the body to give and receive affections, (impressions or imagings) have their mental counterparts in the power to form perceptions or ideas. As bodies differ in their powers to give and receive affections, so do their ideas (minds) differ from one another. For, "ideas like objects, differ one from the other, one being more excellent than another and containing more reality...."(EII,13, Note).

Bodies may be simple or compound. Compound bodies consist of a variable number of parts, each of which may also be simple or compound. Parts within the individual may become greater or less, that is, they may grow or decline. They may also change motion and direction. However, as long as individuals maintain the same mutual relation of motion and rest between the parts, or as long as the overall communication between them remains unchanged, individuals will preseve their original nature and actuality. Thus, "a composite individual may be affected in many different ways, and preserve its nature notwithstanding"(EII,13, Lem.VII, Note). The mental complement of the above is, that the perceptive power of the mind is a correlate of the body's power to receive impressions (EII, 14), and that the constitution of our own body will affect "the ideas that we have of external bodies" (EII, 16, Cor.II).

Each individual is unique. The cross of genetic and environmental factors specific to any given person cannot be duplicated. I am on this earth only once and no more. I am unique, and so are you. "But every man is more than just himself; he also represents the unique, the very special and always significant and remarkable point at which the world's phenomena interact once in this way and never again."[2]

Genetic and environmental differences have their exact complement in the mental sphere. Hereditary differences are determined at the moment of conception. Environmental differences begin right after that, in the womb. From then on, they continue throughout the individual's entire life time. Genetic factors predispose the person in certain ways and the environmental factors may reinforce them, counterbalance them, and act in unspecified ways. This gives an almost unlimited number of possible permutations and combinations by which the genetic and environmental factors may interact, affect, and shape individual existence. Individual differences express themselves in elemental energy levels (motion and rest), in their intensities (quickness and slowness), and in their evolution and direction (environmental impacts and learning processes). Throughout all such changes in development, in growth or in decline, the relation between parts within individuals (subsystems of motion and rest) remain the same. Thereby individuals retains their nature, and actuality. Spinoza incorporates movement and change as well as learning experiences within his deterministic model. During the process of bodily change, individual parts will change absolutely but not relatively. The energy components of individual parts (proportion of motion and rest) may change in absolute terms, but not in relation to each other, which means that they retain the same proportion between them. This assures the unity and identity of the individual throughout the process of change. Individual parts may also undergo proportionate change in varying directions bringing about a greatly expanded and multiplaced possibility of change (EII,16, Lem. VII, Note).

We may conceive an individual composed of many individuals, each of whom undergoes different proportionate change. Thus, the number of ways that an individual can change without losing his nature (identity) "will be greatly multiplied" (EII,13, Lem. VII, Note). We may extend this to infinity, "and conceive the whole nature as one individual, whose parts, that is, all bodies, vary in infinite ways, without any change in the individual as a whole" (Ibid, Note). This implies that the actuality of nature, its identity, stays the same, despite the changes taking place within it all the time.

This is not a crude determinism. The individual's actions are not in any sense given beforehand. But causes exist for our actions, most of which we are not aware. Causes, not our will determine our actions. The difference between ideas (some are more excellent than others), and the difference between minds, (some are more powerful than others), reflect the differences between their objects, (their bodies). Thus, "in proportion as a given body can perform many actions or receive many simultaneous impressions, and the more its actions depend on itself alone, the more fitted is the mind in forming many simultaneous perceptions and in its ability for distinct comprehension"(EII, 13,Note). This explains why some minds are better (more powerful, more excellent) than others. Excellence of mind is a function of quickness or slowness in the body, energy waves and their intensities. This can be greatly enhanced by praxis. Thus, "the intellect, by its native strength, makes for itself intellectual instruments, whereby it acquires strength for performing other intellectual operations, and from these operations gets again fresh instruments, or the power of pushing its investigations further, and thus gradually proceeds till it reaches the summit of wisdom."[3]

The linkage of the mind to the body is not to be interpreted in terms of body fitness or acrobatics. The mind is a correlate of the entire body. It reflects the body's energies in the entire nervous (neuromuscular) system. It does not relate to any particular bodily performance feat. The degree of fitness of one part, such as, muscular strength, gymnastics or athletics may be counterbalanced by slowness in another part (brain waves). Similarly, a paralyzed body may be more than offset by heightened brain functioning (energy waves) or other bodily energies. Thus, a slow moving body, partially or completely paralyzed, will not on that account necessarily have less simultaneous impressions, or less adequate perceptions and comprehension.

4. Consciousness and Self-Consciousness

We arrive at what Spinoza meant by his basic notion of an idea. Spinoza's idea is to be used both in the sense of concept, an abstract idea, as well as of a correlate of an *ideatum*. An abstract idea can only be used by a complex mind reflecting a highly complex body. Thus, any abstract concept, or a universal, would be part of the complex idea of the human mind which corresponds to the complexity of the human body. Such abstract concepts do not correspond to anything that actually exists. They are convenient devices for description and classification of things. "They are and can be entertained only by conscious beings, and consciousness (cogitatio) is always idea as counterpart of body."[4] All ideas are rooted in the immediate awareness of the body, and all ideas are part of the idea of my body.

Consciousness is the reflection of the idea of the body. It is the idea of idea. Self-consciousness is the self-reflection of the mind as the composite idea of the body. The idea is the object of consciousness, as the mind is the object of self-consciousness. Life is essentially mental, whether conscious or not. All mental processes (and all inner life, such as, perceiving, valuing, willing, and reflecting) are object oriented. They are intentional. This intentionality is according to Husserl the most universal characteristic of consciousness. Suppose, I say, my mind is totally empty. Not a single idea is in it. Then this emptiness is what I am conscious of. Thus, all consciousness is necessarily the consciousness of something. This agrees with Spinoza's definition of desire as *conatus* made conscious. When we have an idea of something and we know that we have it, we are obviously conscious of it. Not all consciousness needs to be reflective. It can be unreflective. The unreflective consciousness simply deals with givens or facts. It does not add anything to them. For example, it rains outside, period. However, when I think of the rain (how long it will last, whether I should take an umbrella or not, etc.), I move to a higher level of consciousness, to reflection. Factual awareness takes place on the level of perception. Facts by themselves are meaningless. Mere facts do not reveal to us anything pertaining to their true nature. Everybody who has witnessed two cars crashing into each other will agree that a two car accident or collision occurred. But beyond this most elementary level of perception, people will disagree. They will disagree about the causes of the acccident, the conditions of the road, the visibility, about whose error it was. Thus we move from the level of sheer facts (unreflective consciousness) to the level of analysis and reflective consciousness. On this level, the simplicity and certainty of the facts becomes less subject to simple affirmation or denial. Nevertheless, in terms of the truth content of any idea (statement), affirmation or denial does hold, since an idea is either true or false.

All consciousness is submerged in the unconscious. We are only conscious of our affections. We think through our bodily affections. They are the cause of our consciousness. Through them, the human mind actively conceives ideas. "By idea I understand a conception of the mind which the mind forms because it is a thinking thing"(EII, Def.3). The mind's power of perception is directly related to the sensitivity of the body. Since one is the correlate of the other, the greater the complexity of the body, the greater the complexity of the mind. Since the mind animates the body, and since the mind pervades all of nature (from the most simple to the most complex), all of the universe is animated in some degree.

Consciousness relates to thought as body relates to extension. Just as extension is the ground of body, so is thought the ground of consciousness. Thus, the potential for thought in consciousness (conscious thought) is great. If we take, for the sake of simplicity, the brain as the physical counterpart to potential thought, it is well established that people use a small part of their brain, while the rest of the brain remains undeveloped but subject to potential use. Thus, "no one has hitherto laid down the limits to the powers of the body"(EIII, 2, Sch.), and correspondingly, no one knows the limits of the powers of human mind. The human potential is almost unimaginable. Spinoza stresses the possibilities inherent in the realization of human potential. The essence of man (self- preservation and self-elevation) embraces these possibilities. It is not possible to miss the link between Spinoza's community of free human beings and Marx's vision of a future communist society of associated producers. The line from Spinoza to Marx is direct and unmistakable. The realization of the human potential depends on the optimization of the conditions for its occurrence.

Consciousness means to be conscious of our thoughts (ideas, feelings, volitions). How does this relate to thought as an attribute of God? Is God conscious of his thoughts? Joachim thinks that God is self conscious. "God... is aware of himself and all that follows from himself: and since all consciousness involves self-consciousness, since in thinking or knowing we necessarily know that we know, God is aware of his own thinking: or is self conscious in the sense that he is conscious of his consciousness of himself."[5] In support of this, Joachim cites EII,21,Schol., where Spinoza says that "if a man knows anything, he, by that very fact, knows that he knows it..."[6] Joachim fails to differentiate between substance as the ground of thought and the infinite intellect as the immediate and infinite modification of essence in the attribute of thought. The infinite intellect is self-conscious, but the ground (substance) is not. Joachim errs in applying man's consciousness to God. He also errs in ascribing a self to God. A self implies a not-self and for God the two are the same. God is not conscious of his thoughts since God's thoughts are infinite. For God, consciousness would be a determination and thereby a negation. Only the human mind singles out an idea (or any conceivable succession of ideas), and is conscious of it. To be conscious of a particular idea is a determination (or limitation) in the realm of thought. This is so because a particular idea is singled out for consciousness relative to all the other ideas of which I am not conscious. I am thereby limiting my thought (idea, feeling, desire,) to that idea or desire of which I am conscious. Clearly, this kind of consciousness cannot be applied to God. To God this is all irrelevant, since all ideas are in God and God does not single out any idea for his consciousness. Therefore, Spinoza's God is neither conscious nor self-conscious. Consciousness necesarily implies unconsciousness, and we would be equally absurd to apply it to God. Thus , while Spinoza's God is a thinking thing, and while thought is an Attribute and power of God, God's power of thought is infinite, and God cannot (is not, need not) be conscious of his thoughts or of his power. God and his thoughts (his powers) are one and the same. Thus, the God of Spinoza, (Nature or Substance) is not self conscious. God is not conscious of being God or the world (Nature). God is not a conscious God.

Notes

1. *The Philosophical Works of Descartes,* Translated by Elizabeth S.Haldane and G.R.T.Ross, Vol. I, Cambridge University Press, 1970. p.190.
2. Herman Hesse, *Demian.* NewYork and Evanston: Harper & Row Publishers, 1965. p.2.
3. Errol E. Harris, *Salvation From Despair:* The Hague: Martinus Nijhoff, 1973. p.85.
4. Benedict De Spinoza, *On the Improvement of the Understanding,* Elwes transl. p. 12.
5. Harold H. Joachim, A Study of the Ethics of Spinoza. Oxford: Clarendon Press, 1901. p.72.
6. Ibid.

CHAPTER 3
SPINOZA'S THEORY OF KNOWLEDGE
APPLIED TO THE SELF

1. The First Kind of Knowledge

Spinoza's theory of knowledge is concerned primarily with external reality. It does not deal, initially or principally with what we know about ourselves and how we come to know it, that is, with our internal reality. The three levels of knowledge are arranged in an ascending order, from sense experience (first level) to science (second level) and then to intuition (the third and highest level of knowing).

The body is the principle medium by which we come to know the external world. Objects affect our body through imagings (imprints or affections) that the body receives and emits in its interaction with other objects. For each bodily affection, there is a corresponding mental affection (idea). Affections, imprints, or imagings, is what we get from our senses. The ideas that reflect them are our imaginations about the outside world. Our senses however, do not give us a "true" view of the things outside. They tend to deceive us. For example, the same object will appear large or small depending whether we view it from a distance or from close up. The distant perception is not in itself erroneous, provided that we know, from the study of optics, why it appears small. Failing that, we will get a distorted view of things from our senses.

Sense perceptions and the ideas that correspond to them are for the most part fragmented and disconnected. When the mind "perceives things after the common order of nature" (EII, 29, Corrol.), it does so because it receives its modifications (affections or ideas) "from particular things represented to our intellect fragmentarily, confusedly and without order through our senses" (EII, 40, Note 2).

Besides sense experience, we derive our knowledge also from signs and symbols around which we form ideas which we retain in memory. Such ideas are similar to those based on imagination. Spinoza says: "I shall call both these ways of regarding things knowledge of the first kind, opinion or imagination" (ibid.).

Due to the fragmentary nature of our external perceptions, sense experience cannot be a source of true knowledge. Our ideas do not correspond to their *ideata*. That means that they do not possess "the intrinsic determinations of a true idea" (EII, Def. 4). Spinoza defines an adequate idea as one whereby the essential properties of its *ideatum* can be deduced from it. He gives as an example the idea of a triangle, from which all its properties can be deduced.

When we form and associate ideas with their objects, our mind is largely passive. It reflects external causes acting on us. Nevertheless, empirical knowledge and experience provide a necessary starting point for knowing. We can derive true knowledge by applying correctives to our confused perceptions. Sense perceptions are basic to our ability to know the external world. "Empirical reality is the ultimate source of knowledge and the medium is the human body."[1] It is however deficient when taken by itself. Our experience needs to be corrected and remedied by the true light of reason.

Spinoza's theory of truth unites the correspondence and the coherence theories. The coherence theory allows for truth to be partial and relative. Truth has to be relevant to something else. For example, I am writing this sentence down. I know this to be true. But that is not all the truth about me, my activity, my pen, the paper, and the table. However, we do not need to know all this in order to confirm the fact that right now, I am writing this sentence. It means that truth has to be relevant to the purpose and the circumstance. If someone wants to know what I am doing right now, the answer that I am writing my thoughts down is a true statement. However, if someone would like to know the color of my table, the fact that I am writing would be irrelevant.

For truth to be relevant means that it cannot be closed. It must open avenues for further thought and activity. In line with the coherence theory, even a partial truth opens the way to further truth. Some truths are more basic than other. The truth about a person's character is a more basic truth than the truth about his or her appearance. We have much more difficulty at getting to the more basic truth than to the less basic truth. What often appears to be true is least likely to be true. Appearances are true if they are taken for what they are (appearances). They are not true, if they are taken for what they are not, namely, as an indication of some basic truth. Appearances tend to be deceptive. They are often designed to hide rather than reveal a more basic truth (cosmetics, con artists).

No idea when taken by itself is false. It is inadequate if it is disconnected from the system of causes in nature. The less connected it is, the less adequate or true would the idea be. And conversely, the more connected a given idea is to the overall system of causation, the more adequate (true) would it be. An adequate or true idea will always correspond to its *ideatum*. A onenes of all truth exists within the multiple hierarchies and pyramids of truth. This onenes to which all truth is related and from which all truths emanate is the essence of substance. All existential essences derive this truth from it. To know the truth about oneself that is basic to all other truth is to solve the riddle of the dictum "know thyself."

2. Spinoza's Second Kind of Knowledge

In Spinoza's knowledge of the second kind, the truth of the ideas does not depend on particular bodily modifications or affections. Ideas are inherently true if they are based on notions common to all things and they correspond to "common properties of things". Examples of these are ideas of extension, motion, form, and shape. In forming such notions, the mind is active, and it does not depend on external causes or the senses.

Common notions are equally deduced from the part and from the whole since, "they are equally in the part and in the whole", and "they do not constitute the essence of any particular thing" (EII, 37). Therefore, we have no need to derive these ideas from the experience of particular objects. They are common to all human beings (EII, 38, Cor.). These are the basic principles of geometry, physics, and logic. They are the basis of scientific knowledge and deductive reasoning *(ratio)*. The various disciplines of the sciences are based on these common notions *(ratio)* and therefore they are ontically true.

3. Knowledge of the Third Kind

The third and highest kind of knowledge is knowledge from intuition. This kind of knowledge arrives at the essence of things. It proceeds "from an adequate idea of the absolute essence of certain attributes of god to the adequate knowledge of the essence of things" (EII, 40, Note 2). Through intuition we get to know the essence of particular things. This essence we cannot know from comon notions. This is so because common notions are common to all things and therefore do not reveal the essence of particular things. Intuitive knowledge penetrates into a depth that science can never reach. This is where metaphysics fulfills and complements science. However, in order to arrive at knowledge of the third kind, we must first acquire knowledge of the second kind. We cannot jump over the sequence of cognitive knowledge. Science and *ratio* are preliminaries and a stepping stone to intuition. We cannot go directly from a confused perception to the essence of a thing. The essence of a thing must be preceded by scientific knowledge of bodies in general. Such general knowledge must be ultimately grounded (ontologically) in God. From the idea of God, (the idea of the whole, or the idea of Being), we get to the idea of individual essence. We have to train and discipline our mind, through the use of *ratio* and the second level of knowledge, in order to get to the essence of things. Neither the senses nor the sciences alone can give us this. While the senses give us access to possible knowledge, and while reason gives us access to knowledge in general that is adequate and true, only through intuition can we know the essence of God and the whole of nature. From this we can derive and know the essence of individual bodies.

Essences of individual things must be conceived as necessary, since they are derived from God's essence. They are therefore not contingent. The imagination conceives things as contingent. To conceive things as necessary is to conceive them "under a certain form of eternity" (EII, 44, Cor. 2), and thus to conceive them in relation to God. This is so, since "every idea of every body, or of every particular thing actually existing, necessarily involves the eternal and infinite essence of God" (EII, 45). By existence, Spinoza here means not duration, but "the force whereby each particular thing perseveres in existing". That force can only be attributed to the "eternal necessity of God's nature" (ibid., Note).

The universe of particular modes, where each particular thing is conditioned to exist by another particular thing, and so on ad infinitum, is in its entirety (as *Natura naturata*) grounded in God (as *Natura naturans*). To have an adequate idea of anyone thing, ultimately necessitates the understanding of the whole, that is, the idea of God. Truth is in God (in the whole), and from it we get the truth of individual things. Only such truth is adequate. The human mind is, according to Spinoza, capable of arriving at an adequate knowledge "of the eternal and infinite essence of God" (EII, 47). This represents the highest kind of knowledge. In this knowledge, the mind reaches the highest level of activity.

4. The Truth About the Self

Most of what we know or think about ourselves is based on self-perception. As such, it is comparable to Spinoza's first kind of knowledge. However, it is likely to be even more distorted, confused, and inadequate than our knowledge of external reality which we get from sense experience. The reason for this is, the bias that is built in us in our favor. We want to look good to ourselves and to others.

When we talk about self-knowledge, we are talking about our mental states, which necessarily reflect our bodily states. Descartes' separation of mind and body and their independent existence is immediately rejected by Spinoza. "The object of our mind is the body as it exists, and nothing else" (EII, 13, Schol.). Contrary to Descartes, no such thing exists as a mind without a body or vice versa. Spinoza does not establish the priority of the body over the mind (Prop.13 in EII), he simply denies the possibilty of one without the other.

Our mental states (ideas in our mind) represent or correspond to modifications (affections) of our body. Our consciousness is based on the consciousness of our body. All modifications and affections of our body, from the time of our birth, have had their exact mental counterparts in ideas. Imagine what that does to the nature of our consciousness. Most of these impressions are deeply buried in our unconscious state. This may illustrate why our conscious state represents only the tip of an iceberg. To be self-conscious is to be conscious of the ideas of our bodily impressions and modifications, that is, to have ideas of ideas. Thus, "the human mind does not know itself, except in so far as it perceives the ideas of the modifications of the body" (EII, 23). What we know, are our bodily modifications or affections expressed as ideas. Since our ideas relate to individual affections, or impressions, it therefore follows, that "the idea of each modification of the human body does not involve an adequate knowledge of the human body itself" (EII, 27). Such ideas are by and large confused ideas. We do not get adequate knowledge of our physical self from the ideas of the modifications of our body, that is, from self-perception. Similarly, we don't have adequate knowledge of our mental self or of our mind. This is expressed by Spinoza in EII, Prop.29: "The idea of the idea of each modification of the human body does not involve an adequate knowledge of the human mind." In as much as our ideas represent diverse bodily affections, and the ideas of these ideas represent corresponding mental states, we cannot have adequate knowledge either of our mind or of our body. What we think of ourselves and of our mental states (feelings, etc.) will for the most part be distorted, confused, and inadequate. It forms part of our imagination and it constitutes thereby not truth but fiction.

5. An Illustration From Everyday Experience: Consider the Question of "How Do I Know What I Want To Do?"[2]

Most people think that they know what they want or would like to do, if they only had the freedom to do what they want. However, when confronted with the question directly, they are baffled to find out that they really don't know the "true" answer to this question. Why is this so? The answer is complex. It is a reflection of our past life, and therefore, everything of what we did, how we did things and what we failed but hoped to do (our wishes, dreams, frustrations), as well as what we thought we were expected to do by those significant others in our life. All these conscious and unconscious manifestations of our past, bear significantly on the answer to this simple question of why it is that most of us don't really know what we want, and correspondingly, why we don't know what we would really want to do.

The fact that we are caught by surprise when confronted with this question directly and openly, indicates that we didn't really want to deal with it, and, perhaps we were afraid to face it and thus admit to ourselves our basic lack of determination in the pursuit of internalized goals that we have not been made explicit to ourselves. In a way, it is a reflection of a lack of courage or faith in our ability to pursue and achieve what we really want. As long as we don't need to confront it or face up to it, the dream and and the wish and the hope and the illusion, they all remain with us, and our concrete reality, the work which we don't enjoy too much, the relationships that don't work out to well, the mechanics of daily life, all of these are easier to endure, if there is this romantic side to us, which somehow gives slight comfort and perhaps strength to carry on, despite all.

Thus, a simple confrontation in terms of what we want to do with ourselves, what we want for ourselves, and what kind of work would open up the creative aspects of our buried productive potential, could have a sobering and more lasting effect on us. There is this initial surprise of not knowing the answer to this seemingly simple question (what do I want?) while, all the while we were acting on the expressed or apparent premise that we knew what we want (" if I only could do what I want or always wanted to do.") The initial surprise that we have been going through life on a false premise of knowing ourselves, while the truth was that of not knowing ourselves, will come as a shock to some people, especially to those who have gotten into the habit of concealing things from themselves and who have perfected the art of self-deception.

The above example clearly illustrates Spinoza's "knowledge of the first kind," as applied to the self. The idea that "we know what we want to do" is largely a distorted and confused idea. It reflects our bodily interactions and affections together with their corresponding mental states (ideas) of our entire past. We carry around such inadequate and fictitious ideas about ourselves all the time. We could recite a whole catalogue of aspects of self-knowledge, such as, our beliefs, values, expectations, attitudes, and character traits, and we will find ourselves in the dark with respect to every one of them, most of the time, if not all of the time. This conforms to Spinoza's proposition that the mind does not have "an adequate knowledge of itself" (EII, 24), nor of its own body (EII, 27), nor of external bodies (EII, 25), but a fragmentary and confused knowledge thereof" (EII, 38, Note and II, 29, Corol.).

What we think about ourselves is largely a matter of what others (or the significant others) think about us. This knowledge of ourselves is shaped by the signals of approval or disapproval that we pick up through our bodies from others in our daily interactions with them. The same holds true of our knowledge of others. Our perceptions of others are largely based on what we consciously and subconsciously think of ourselves. They represent the constitution of our body and the ideas of its modifications as reflected to others, that is, they are images, imagings, or imaginations received and projected. If all of this seems circular, it is because it is circular. We live in the world where we continuously affect and are affected by others. All such ideas (about ourselves and others) are therefore distorted and confused. Throughout most of this, our mind is not active, but passive. This is so, because our ideas are largely based on fiction rather than understanding. Once we realize the fictitious nature of our self-perception, we may actively engage our mind to understand ourselves. Only then will we move toward self- knowledge. This is the journey from ignorance about the self (from self-knowledge of the first kind) to self-discovery (and to self-knowledge of the second kind).

6. The Truth About the Self: The Second Level of Self- Knowledge. A Movement From Lower to Higher Levels of Reality or Self-Perception

Self-knowledge of the second kind is based on "common notions," on what is common to all people rather than, on what is peculiar and distinct to each one. Common to all human beings is the faculty of reason and the possibility of being aware of the true causes of our erroneous perceptions. Hence, to move from the first to the second level of knowledge about the self, we must overcome our subjectivity. Given the uniqueness of each person, our unique experience, background and the limited freedom within which we operate, this movement toward the truth about the self is not easy or common. A time may come when we are compelled by force of circumstance to confront ourselves and to look for the true causes of our behavior.

The self-confrontation of what we wanted to do, revealed to us that we really didn't know it, while we have always assumed that we knew what we wanted to do most. With the comfort of this self-deceptive illusion gone, we may now begin to introspect and search for our real interests. We may soon find out that interests are not something given. We will understand that interests must be created, developed, renewed, cultivated, and nurtured. To have interests means to be interested, it means to actively engage ourselves in life, in whatever form. To be interested means to be engaged. This can only be developed by practice. We cannot expect to have interests without the practice of self-involvement whose effect is the development of interests.

Before we have interests we have inclinations. These are not differentiated. We might be inclined to do one thing or another. We choose to do this rather than that. As a result, we evolve an interest in what we do. The first thing in examining our interests, is to become engaged in the things we do. To be engaged is the first step in the process of self-discovery, in this case, the discovery of our inclinations. Self-engagement means to be fully concentrated on the activity at hand. It means to give ourselves fully to the experience of the moment. For example, if I have a conversation with another person, I have to practice being fully engaged with the other person in my listening, concentrating, and focusing my attention fully onto the other. Or, suppose I meet someone I know. We may be talking to each other, but my mind may be somewhere else. The other person might not notice that I am distracted. He or she continues telling me of something that happened the day before, and I may go on pretending that I am listening. Such encounters with acquaintainces will reflect on ourselves as well as on the other person in relation to ourselves. We are unable to engage ourselves fully with the other person, because we are too self-preoccupied and too self-centered.

Through the confrontation of ourselves with what we want to do, we were able to break through our self-deception. This may just be a one time event, or it may be the beginninng of an effort at self-discovery. This process of finding ourselves through the overcoming of ourselves (our subjectivity) entails the active pursuit of truth and the love of truth. We love the truth even if it is painful, which is most often the case *(amor fati)*.

A significant part of the search for truth involves clearing the path of truth rather than finding it. This is a process of deconditioning, a shaking loose of the chains of our past that have rigidified our ways of thinking and acting. It does not consist of reaching the one and only truth about the self. We cannot be apodictic about our real self. The process and the outcome, the self and its truth are continuously evolving. In line with the Heisenberg uncertainty principle, the process of reaching the truth may alter the truth itself. It is not the absolute truth that Spinoza's knowledge of the second kind seeks, when applied to the self.

Fixed behavior and thought patterns inhibit our ability to fully involve ourselves in life. They stand in the way of living and enjoying life fully. The process of releasing our fixations and of opening up the locked-in ways of thinking, acting, and relating, involves a readiness to look at ourselves objectively instead of subjectively. It is the ability to look at ourselves from outside in, rather than from inside out. It involves the overcoming of our self-centeredness. It requires a mental effort, normally precipitated by some bodily crisis, to get at the bottom of ourselves. Unfortunately, this is not a one-time thing. It is a life long process, a journey into ourselves that never ends. It is a journey with an aim but without a destination. We need courage to embark on it, and courage is also one of its byproducts. Everything that is difficult in life becomes less difficult the second time around. By acquiring insight into ourselves (true ideas about the self), we perfect our intellectual instruments that will ultimately enable us to reach the "summit of wisdom."[3]

7. Knowledge of the Third Kind: Intuition into the Essence of Things

Spinoza explains the third kind of knowledge as "when a thing is perceived solely through its essence, or through the knowledge of its proximate cause." As an example of this kind of knowledge, he cites, "from knowing the essence of the mind, I know that it is united to the body."[4] In the *Ethics*, Spinoza refers to the third kind of knowledge as intuition and he defines it as proceeding "from an adequate idea of the absolute essence of certain attributes of God to the adequate knowledge of the essence of things" (EII, 40, Note 2). Also, "The human mind has an adequate knowledge of the eternal and infinite essence of God" (EII, 47). The third kind of knowledge proceeds from the essence of God to the essence of things. "Now as all things are in God, and are conceived through God, we can from this knowledge infer many things, which we may adequately know"(EII, 47, Sch.). This knowledge of particular things is inferred from the knowledge of God (intuitive knowledge), and is more potent and more powerful than the universal knowledge "which I have styled knowledge of the second kind" (EV, 36, Note). These quotations show that intuitive knowledge pertains to the knowledge of the essence of things. Such knowledge cannot be arrived at through science. Science can only explain properties of things but not their essence. Intuition does not circumvent science and reason. Reason is a necessary prerequisite for intuition, and knowledge of the second kind necessarily precedes knowledge of the third kind. Intuition is not a substitute for reason, but it is its complement and fulfillment. But we must know what we mean by the "essence" of things.

Essence *(essentia)* derives from the word *esse,* to be. It has usually been taken as a noun, to indicate the innermost quality of a thing, or what makes the thing be what it is (the whatness of a thing). Thus, we can never see the essence of a thing with our senses (even when improved and perfected by reason and science). We can only perceive the thing's manifestations. The innermost quality of a thing, its essence, can only be conceived through intuition. A direct correlation exists between the degree or nature of perception (understanding, knowledge, internalizations of perceptions,) and intuition. The greater the degree of real understanding of anything (subject, event, person) the more likely will be the complementary extension of such knowledge through intuition.

Intuition is as much a function of the extent (breadth) of knowledge, as it is of the depth of knowledge and its integration with experience. The essential integration and comprehension of knowledge (the internalization of knowledge) is of primary importance with respect to intuition. Knowledge must turn into an inner experience, an all-absorbing activity, in order for us to develop our intuitive ability. All intuition is strictly personal and subjective. Yet its insight pertains to the outside (and inner) world, that is objective and real, but hidden from direct perception through the senses, or from the availability of measurable and quantifiable (empirical) data.

No absolute break occurs between perception and intuition. Visible perception gradually extends itself into the realm of the invisible. We often associate art with intuition, and we think of the artist as having a greater than ordinary ability to intuit. We may also think of intuition as what distinguishes the arts from the sciences. We make a crude distinction between the two. True science and true art necessarily merge together and become one. When artists extend their vision into science and when scientists turn their science into art, they have both transcended their own boundaries and reached a higher level of knowing. They experience higher levels of intuition and creativity. The further scientists reach into the inner depth of their subject matter, and the more they reach into the inner yet unknown layers of knowledge, they get this illumination from intuition.

Every scientific hypothesis rests on intuition. Since all progress in the sciences and in all other areas takes initially the form of hypotheses that need to be independently verified, all advances in human knowledge are ultimately linked to intuition. Intuition helps us extend the scope of our empirical knowledge, but it alone can give us an understanding of the essence of things.

So far, we have taken the essence to mean the inner core of a thing or its "whatness." In this way, we denote the essence as the "being" of a thing. This is the traditional meaning of essence. Suppose however, that we take the meaning of *essentia* in terms of its *esse*, to be. That makes essence an innermost quality of the thing's existence or of its durational being. We can immediately differentiate here between two meanings of essence: (1) the nondurational aspect of essence, the unchanging core of a thing, and (2) the durational or existential aspect of essence, the essence of the thing's existence. The one is to be conceived under the aspect of eternity *(sub species aeternitatis)*, the other, under the aspect of time *(sub species durationis)*. In God there is no such distinction, because essence and existence are the same. The distinction holds true only for finite modes with respect to human beings. Therefore, we can legitimately ask the question about the meaning of our essence (our connection to nature and God), and the meaning of the essence of our existence (our connection to what it means "to be" with respect to the time alloted to us on this earth.) In the first sense, the finite is grounded in the infinite (we depend on God for our being), and in the other sense, each invidual may forever strive to express his or her unique essence in their existence. Most commentators feel that Spinoza considers essence in the first sense, but Wienpahl[5]thinks that Spinoza's essence refers to Being in time, namely, a dynamic, moving, and existential essence. This is especially so, since freedom (the existential essence of an individual), is viewed by Spinoza as active self-determination. The more individuals are self determined (and active) and the more ways of acting (reality) they have, the more free and the more perfect they are. Spinoza, like Aristotle, regards human activity as the highest good, while the highest activity consists in knowing God which includes knowing the self (self-knowledge). Through intuition we can know our essence as connected to Nature (the union of the mind with the whole of Nature), and we can also ascertain the essence of our existence. An individual is thus in a privileged position with respect to knowing his or her essence. We are both part of nature and apart from nature through our ability to be self-conscious.[6] Our existential essence is the unending desire for the resolution of this conflict, namely to be one with nature and to lose our separatedness from our fellow human beings.

Notes

1. C. De Deugd, *The Significance of Spinoza's First Kind of Knowledge.* Assen, Netherlands: Van Gorcum, 1966. p.253.
2. "To know what one really wants is one of the most difficult problems that anyone has to solve" Eric Fromm , *The Escape from Freedom,* Avon Books, 1967. p.252. See also Nietzsche, "What am I really doing and why am I doing it"?, in *Daybreak: Thoughts on the Prejudices of Morality.* New York: Cambridge University Press, 1982. p.117.
3. Benedict De Spinoza, *On the Improvement of the Understanding,* Elwes Transl. p.12. In the context of the self, "the summit of wisdom" is self-knowledge.
4. Ibid., p.9.
5. Paul Wienpahl, *The Radical Spinoza.* New York: New York University Press, 1979.
6. Eric Fromm, *The Heart of Man, Its Genius for Good and Evil.* New York: Perennial Library, 1971.

CHAPTER 4
THE EXISTENTIAL PROBLEM OF
SELF-KNOWLEDGE

1. The Mind's Control over the Emotions

Only through understanding can the mind control the emotions. Understanding involves both the proper identification of the emotion and the knowledge of its proximate cause. Our emotions are an integral part of the general order of nature. They are subject to its universal laws and rules. Every emotion has a cause through which it can be understood. The contemplation of the true causes of our emotion fills us with delight. We rejoice in the knowledge of the truth of our being. This power of the transition to a higher level of reality (and perfection) along with the consequent feeling of pleasure and joy derived from it can restrain and control our passions.

We cannot control our emotions by the power of our will, as the Stoa assumed, nor by the power of our reason, as St. Thomas and the Schoolmen assumed, "An emotion can only be displaced by a contrary emotion that is stronger than itself" (EIV, 7 and Schol.). The mind's power over the emotions is derived from the blessedness (joy) of its understanding of the highest reality (God). We do not rejoice because we control our emotions. We control our emotions because we rejoice in the understanding of the truth. It is through the intuitive knowledge of God by the third level of knowledge that we rejoice in the truth (EV, 42).

The joy of knowing the truth extends equally to self- understanding. The truth of self-understanding is more powerful in its delight of knowing than the power of the negative emotions that it reveals. Gaining adequate knowledge of the proximate causes of our emotions enhances our power of self- preservation and our freedom of self-determination. It enlarges the power of activity in our body and the power of our thought in our mind (EIII, 3 and 11). It signifies the transition to a higher level of reality or perfection. The transition to a higher level of reality or perfection is a source of pleasure and joy.

Emotions (modifications of our body) are activities (active) to the extent that we are their adequate cause. This is only the case when we understand our emotions. Otherwise, they are passions (EIII, Def.3). The joy of knowing is derived from the knowledge of the self as the adequate cause of its affections. The self's power of activity is enhanced thereby. "When the mind regards itself and its own power of activity, it feels pleasure..." (EIII, 53).

The question of the extent to which the mind has the power to restrain the emotions is essentially the question of whether and to what extent we have the power to control ourselves and our passions. We do not have absolute power over our actions, but the mind has the power to restrain our emotions. This power lies in the feeling of delight and joy that true understanding of our passions brings about. Unfortunately, such self-understanding (and the ensuing joy thereof), is not a common occurrence. More often than not, we act compulsively, whereby we are prey to our emotions. Man is not his own master, "but lies at the mercy of fortune: so much so, that he is often compelled, while seeing that which is better for him, to follow that which is worse" (EIV, Preface). We do not on the whole act rationally. Neither reason (self-interest) nor the will can give us power over our emotions. Such power can be derived only from our ability to understand ourselves.

Freud was not the first to discover that man is not the master of his own house, (i.e. the ego does not control the id). Long before him Spinoza entitled Part Four of his Ethics "Of Human Bondage." Freud nevertheless insisted[1] that he was the first one to come out with this discovery and he used this to explain the animosity with which his ideas were received by the then prevailing literary and medical establishment. He compared his revolutionary discovery to the Copernican and Darwinian revolutions in Western thought. The Copernican revolution removed the Earth (man's abode) from the center of the universe and assigned to it a common place among the other planets orbiting the sun. The Darwinian revolution showed man to be descendent from lower level creatures, rather than to have been made in the image of God. Finally, the Freudian revolution showed that man is not even the master of his own house. All three revolutions deflated man and his place in the universe, among the living creatures and within himself. They ran counter to the established cultural and religious attitudes of the time. These considered man to be the center of God's creation and "to be situated in nature as a kingdom within a kingdom" (EIII, Opening statement).

All three revolutionary discoveries met with great resistance and animosity. By this official hostility Freud was reinforced in the truth of his ideas and was able to compare himself to his two famous predecessors Copernicus and Darwin. One might add here, that Spinoza too, and for the same reasons, also encountered great hostility from the then established religious and literary authorities.

Spinoza believed that man, by the power of his thinking and introspection, can arrive at the knowledge of his mental states, his bodily affects, and the proximate causes of his emotions. This presupposes the proper identification of the nature of the affects and the awareness of their causes. Both of these are at the basis of the question of man's need to find himself. Their quest however is laden with difficulties and is subject to error. Yet, the resolution of the question of our being is the fundamental question of our existence. It is precisely the question of finding ourselves. If individuals are able to resolve this question early in life, they will find themselves at an advantage. But, even in the other extreme, when many of life's options have been foreclosed by circumstance of age, it is equally important to know our essence. This will save us from despair.

2. The Existential Problem of "Finding Ourselves" or of Knowing Our Real Self

The notion of the "real" self is not meant to be contrasted or opposed to the "unreal" self. All of the self is obviously real, regardless whether it consists of adequate or inadequate ideas about itself. "Real" versus "unreal" merely denotes having more reality or less reality, not whether they have existence. The terms "real" and "unreal" have found their place in colloquial usage, when we refer to someone who means what he or she says as "being for real," while otherwise we call the person unreal (or phony).

To the extent that we are the adequate cause of our affects, our active bodily and mental powers are increased. In the opposite case, when we are not the adequate cause of our emotions, our mind is passive and such emotions are called passions (EIII, Def.3). Different things affect our self-perceptions at different times. We are affected by our transient or momentary feelings, by the way we perceive ourselves (our self-image), by our more stable character traits, and by our subconscious desires. Each of these may be adequate or inadequate. We may mislabel our feelings, we may misread our character, and we may misconceive our desires and our self- image. The greater the deviation between our "true" mental states and our subjective perception of them, the greater will be the distortion of our awareness of ourselves and of the outside world. The less distortion in our ideas about ourselves and about others, the closer we get to our real self. Again, the real self needs to be interpreted as the reaching of higher levels of reality with respect to ourselves. The transition from a less real to a more real mental state is the same as attaining a degree of freedom from self-deception. This gives us greater power over ourselves. The accompanying emotions will have their causes within us, meaning that we are their adequate cause. We become more self determined and our mind is more active. We reach a greater level of reality (truth or perfection), and we experience thereby feelings of pleasure and joy. The joy is derived from our enhanced self-dependence. The enhanced self-dependence frees our powers to understand, to think, and to act. We reach a more adequate understanding of ourselves. Our self-concept has reached a higher level of perfection. This is true, even if we have to part with some long held cherished illusions or delusions about ourselves.

Let us take a hypothetical example, admittedly extreme. While more typical of an adolescent than of a mature person, it will pinpoint the problem. On the other hand, who can tell how much of the adolescent remains in each of us. Suppose in me is a deep-seated desire to be strong and courageous. Yet often I show weakness and fear in the face of danger. I have developed ways of avoiding danger rather than facing it. I have also developed ways of rationalizing my timidity in order not to have to confront myself. I have learned to live in bad faith. Yet I cannot always run away from myself or hide myself from myself. Whenever I fail to live up to my self-image of being courageous, I feel tension and pain. The conflicting emotions of what I am (weak) and of what I want to be (strong) have a paralyzing effect on me. My power of activity (in body and mind) has been diminished. Now, let us analyze these conflicting emotions more closely.

My desire to be strong and courageous is not based on understanding. It is an irrational desire based on the need for outside approval and perhaps admiration. Whenever I fail to live up to this projected image of physical courage, I experience emotional discomfort and pain. Since my self-image does not reflect my true self, I will be often exposed to emotional pain over which I have no control. The source of this pain comes from the outside, because by revealing my timidity and lack of physical courage I have been caught lying and acting in bad faith. Thus, I am filled with shame. This emotion of shame is propelled by an external and therefore inadequate cause. This is one source of pain. The other source of the negative emotion lies in my lack of understanding of the meaning of strength. Spinoza defines strength of character *(fortitudo)* as actions based on understanding rather than on impulse. He describes strength of character in terms of courage and highmindedness. Actions which are designed solely for the good of the person are attributed to courage. Those which aim for the good of others are attributed to highmindedness. "Thus temperance, sobriety and, presence of mind in danger, etc. are varieties of courage; courtesy, mercy etc. are varieties of highmindedness" (EIII, 59, Note). And, "The free man is as courageous in timely retreat as in combat; or a free man shows equal courage or presence of mind, whether he elects to give battle or to retreat" (EIV. 59, Corr.). Timely retreat is just as much an act of courage as facing the enemy in battle. Here we find the second cause of the emotional distress. It lies in the inadequate understanding of the meaning of courage. My failure to understand that strength of character necessitates that my actions be based on reason rather than on impulse or irrational desire is an additional, external cause for my painful feelings. Due to my lack of understanding, I mistook temperance for weakness and excessive boldness (macho) for courage, while the very opposite is the case. Therefore, when I improve my understanding, I gain greater independence from suffering (I overcome my suffering) and I also gain more freedom.

Increased understanding means that I am the (adequate) cause of my emotions. My power of self-determination is thereby enhanced. My mind is more active, and this transition to a higher level of reality expresses itself in a feeling of pleasure. A renewed sense arises of the possibility to advance to a higher level of real strength that is consistent with my true nature. All of this was previously blocked by my persistent self-denial and by my compulsive clinging to inadequate ideas based on a false self-concept.

Let us give another example that is more common. Suppose I want to project a sense of self-confidence and inner security about myself which I am lacking. In truth, I feel insecure deep inside. This example is similar to the previous one, but it is more general and broader. The desire to project self- confidence is not conscious. This desire will nevertheless affect my actions and behavior without me being able to acquiesce in the true motives or causes for my actions. I will ascribe reasons for my actions which do not reflect an inner truth. They will therefore be false reasons. Yet I cannot completely do away with my awareness of their falsehood. This conflict between the suppressed desire and the inability to live up to it will constitute a permanent source of inner tension. It will thereby inhibit my ability to act freely and in accordance with reason. My actions will tend to be not in my best self- interest. At times they might be self-destructive. The self- destructive nature of my actions will bring about an emotion of pain. The source of the pain is that we are acting against ourselves. We are becoming less real, less well, and more imperfect. Since the causes that operate on us are largely external (the preservation of our false self-image, namely, the desire to be what we are not), our mind is passive in all such actions and behavior. This passivity of the mind comes from our failure to understand the meaning and significance of real self- confidence and inner security, whence, the lower level of reality upon which we are operating. By continuously clinging to this false concept we are underwriting a continuous source of our emotional pain and distress. Once we understand that real self- confidence can only come from self-understanding and self- acceptance, we can confront our irrational desire (to be what I am not) actively. This realization opens us up to ourselves and to the world. We are activating the powers of our mind and we are able to free ourselves from our emotional predicament and from the self-inflicted pain. We become free from the external and inadequate causes of our actions which are the source of our pain. This enhanced self-activity of our mind brings with it a true sense of greater power. It represents a transition from a lower to a higher level of reality and perfection. This transition brings with it an exhilarating feeling of pleasure and inner joy.

The examples can be multiplied at will. Whenever a divergence occurs between the reality of what we are, and the desire of what we want to be, or in other words, whenever we fail to fully accept ourselves, we are bound to experience inner tension arising from our conflicted feelings about ourselves. The intensity of the conflict will parallel the extent of the gap existing betwen the truth of ourselves (our reality) and our unrealistic expectations of ourselves. When we narrow or eliminate the gap, an easing of tension occurs due to the resolution of the conflict. This easing of tension brings with it a feeling of pleasure. We become more real and less inhibited. Things that we formerly could do only with great effort become easy. In this way we gain greater independence and greater power over ourselves. This transition to greater reality and perfection makes us stronger and gives us more power to determine our actions from within ourselves. The ensuing emotions of pleasure and satisfaction are brought about from within, due to internal causes, whereby our mind is active by having adequate ideas of ourselves rather than from without or through external causes.

The examples cited, deal with the gap betwen an illusory self and the reality of our true self. Illusions of whatever nature will always hold us back and prevent us from living our life more fully. However, we might also have a lower or more negative image of ourselves than what our true capabilities would justify. In other words, we may suffer from feelings of inferiority. The overcoming of such a negative self-image will bring with it a greater sense of power and the concomitant transition to a higher level of reality and perfection. Again, this will be a source of joy and pleasure.

The shedding of illusions and the strengthening of our ego, whether by making our aspirations more realistic or by overcoming feelings of inferiority, can only occur gradually and incrementally. We cannot change ourselves in one great flash of insight. Even with understanding, lapses and relapses into former, compulsive ways of behavior are bound to occur, since these make our pain familiar and comfortable to live with. Nevertheless, the possibility for change is given to us. "We may love what we once hated, or be bold where we were once timid" (EIII, 51, Note.) The process of change and personal growth requires time and perseverance. With each instance of self- liberation through real understanding and self-knowledge, all subsequent attempts at self-knowledge and self-determination through freedom become easier.

This does not mean that we have to let go of our dreams, desires or ambitions. To do that would be to let go of our very nature and essence. This is clearly impossible because we would get caught up in an existential

52

contradiction. Only when our unconscious desires hold us back and prevent us from living our life more fully, and only to the extent that they inhibit the free activity of our mind and body, can we free ourselves by bringing these desires into our consciousness and by putting them on a firmer ground of enhanced reality rather than letting them endure on the quicksand of fiction.

3. The Question of Freedom and Self-Determination

We are neither totally free, nor totally determined. We can increase the measure of our freedom by becoming aware of the causes behind our actions. Determinism simply means causation. We are part of the universal order of causation. This eternal system of causes operates in nature and it holds the universe together. We can change our actions only to the extent that we replace conscious causes for the unconscious ones. In this we gain a greater measure of freedom. To the extent that we are unaware of the true causes operating behind our actions, we are determined and unfree. It is exactly the opposite of what we think of ourselves. We think of ourselves as being free because we don't know the true causes behind our actions. Just the opposite constitutes our freedom.

People often confuse determinism with fatalism (we can do nothing to change our destiny.) They also confuse real freedom with spontaneous or absolute freedom. The notion of absolute freedom is behind Kant's freedom in the noumenal sphere. However, both of these notions are misleading.

Some things about us we cannot change, such as our heredity or our past. Both of these will continue to causally affect our present, and through it, determine our future. We can, however, improve our understanding of both. That will enable us to affect within prescribed limits our future actions and their outcomes. In this sense we can say that we have a measure of control over our life. We can change the blind effects of our past through a better understanding of it. We can even affect our heredity through a better understanding and awareness of it. We can control some hereditary tendencies within us by taking preventive or offsetting measures. This practice is well established in the field of medicine. Thus, we retain a measure of freedom even in those areas that seem to be fully enclosed.

This understanding of our past and of our heredity is not the same as freedom of the will. I cannot make anything happen to me by the sheer force of my will. Neither can I will anything that is impossible for me to attain. I cannot control my emotions or make them go away by the force of my will. When I am sick, the force of my will to be healthy will not cure me. Instead, it would most likely retard the natural healing process. Similarly, when I am poor, the will to be rich will not by itself make wealth come about. Will is an aspect of my intellect. By it, I can either affirm or deny an idea. If the idea is unrealistic, inadequate, or fictitious, I may deny it. If it is realistic or possible of attainment, I may embrace it. The latter however is not any more an aspect of my will. It now becomes desire. What reason deems as unreal may still persist as an unconscious desire and thus affect my actions. Desire, says Spinoza, (EIII,9, and EIII, def. of desire) is our endeavor to self-preserve and self-elevate. It is *conatus* made conscious.

Spinoza's reflection about the possible direction of his life, as described in the opening pages of *"Towards the Improvement of the Understanding,"* is precisely an indication of an individual's power to affect and determine the course of his or her life in its broad contours. It takes a superior and more stable character to sort out the priorities in our life from among the conflicting desires and aspirations that impose themselves upon us. Spinoza lists the most common desires that impose themselves upon us as wealth, fame, and sensual pleasure. Most of us are driven by the same desires, but due to the infirmity of our mind, we often lack the courage and the self-honesty to clarify or even reveal our deep-seated desires to ourselves. They seem unattainable because they are often based on our emotions rather than on reason. By our failure to clarify them, they are relegated to the domain of the unconscious, and we thereby become subjected and held in bondage to them. We are perpetuating a state of permanent conflict within ourselves. Since this conflict is not in the open, we cannot resolve it. We thereby remain forever inhibited and hampered in our ability to think clearly about our life's priorities. We find it difficult to discriminate or differentiate between what really matters to us and what is less important. We are prevented from the possibility of giving to ourselves the freedom for authentic self-expression. Hence the need to clarify our basic sense of direction is perhaps the key existential problem that we have to face up to. We need to squarely face the questions of where we are heading, of what we want to do, and of what we want to do with our lives.

Spinoza was able to resolve the question of his being when he was about to reach adulthood. As a young man, he was reflecting on the direction of his life and of whether any single thing exists that would bring him "supreme and unending happiness" if he were to dedicate his life to it. He rejected all conventional goals (fame, riches, and sensual pleasures) as false goals. The goods that most people pursue are transitory and perishable. After the pleasure of their attainment comes the sadness of their loss. Spinoza concluded that "happiness or unhappiness" depend entirely on the quality of the object of our love. When we love a thing that is eternal, we are always filled with joy, and such joy is unmingled with sadness because we can never lose it.

Yet, to give up our desires for wordly goods is not a simple matter. Spinoza noticed that as he was preoccupied with these thoughts, of what would give him supreme and unending happiness, he was able to put aside his ordinary worldly goals and pursuits. He realized that he could turn away from his former objects of desire and look for a new principle to rule his life. He understood that the acquistion of fame, wealth, or sensual pleasures, may hinder rather than advance the good life. This is especially so if these goods are sought as ends instead of means. He realized that only as means are they likely to enhance the person's happiness in the pursuit of his or her real end, which is, to seek the true good or the highest good. He concluded that the true good is to be sought in the acquistion of a stable character "to acquire a human character much more stable than his own." Whatever helps to achieve such a character is to be called good. "The chief good is that we should arrive, together with other individuals if possible, at the possession of the aforesaid character".[2] Such a perfect character is "the knowledge of the union existing between the mind and the whole of nature".[3] In that lies the ultimate happiness of human beings.

Most of us are not capable of attaining such perfection of character. Life, for most people, is an existential struggle for many competing ends. We are propelled by hidden motives and by forces unknown to us into directions that are inimical to our true welfare and lasting happiness. As we struggle to understand those forces, we may slowly liberate ourselves from their grip over us. Through disciplined and honest introspection we can attain and reach higher levels of self-understanding. It necessitates a sorting out of the diverse priorities, the important from the less important ones, that impinge on a given life situation. As we endeavor to conquer our compulsions and ready defenses, we may have to let go of what is familiar and embark on a course that is uncharted. We may have to discard false aims and values that we have pursued over our life time. Yet we cannot expect to fully conquer the darker side in us. All we can do is to persistently try to liberate ourselves from ourselves. This process of self liberation is itself part of our becoming liberated. The road to freedom is already part of our freedom. In this process of becoming more free, our human potential unfolds itself and we are able to exploit more fully the opportunities for love, friendship, creativity, and productive contribution to humanity. As we have indicated, the process of inner freedom involves an overcoming of the illusory self and the need to appreciate and accept our true self with all its strength and limitations. It involves a clearing of the path to self truth by coming to grips with our basic sense of direction. [4] It involves the overcoming of those debilitating character tendencies that strangle our power and freedom to act. It necessitates the bringing into the open and becoming aware of the inner conflicts that inhibit our ability to apply reason as a basis for our actions.

The ultimate purpose of self-renewal is to make us free to determine ourselves. In this sense the ego determines itself. The ego creates and recreates itself in the ongoing process through life. The ultimate meaning of freedom is the freedom to be ourselves. For Spinoza, to be ourselves means to conform to reason. When we get to know ourselves, we are able to assume greater control over our life, and all areas of life become less dificult and more manageable.

Self-renewal leads to the recognition of our truly human needs and true desires. The most basic human needs are to give and receive love, and to live in friendship and peace with others. Generalized human values, such as, kindness, goodness of heart, generosity, highmindedness, and compassion, are the fountainhead of love, "minds are not conquered by force, but by love and highmindedness" (EIV, App., 11).

Respect, trust, and interest in each other are the basis for the cultivating of friendship. "There is no individual thing in nature, which is more useful to man, than a man who lives in obedience to reason" (EIV, 35, Cor.1), "the good which every man, who follows after virtue, desires for himself, he will also desire for other men..." (EIV, 37), "the desire, whereby a man living according to reason is bound to associate others with himself in friendship, I call honour" (EIV, 37, Note 1).

Our true desires are those which spring from reason. Their underlying emotions are always pleasurable. In them, the mind is not passive but active, and the pleasure is never excessive or one-sided.

The process of self-renewal also leads to the recognition of our work as a source of our true well-being. Interest in our work and work projects is the backbone of life. Work ties the individual to society. That is how work is sustained, nourished, renewed, energized, and enjoyed. Work is a shared activity. Everybody needs to share his or her work directly or indirectly with others. Clarity about our work and work-related concerns is a counterdose to anxiety. Anxiety prevents the person from recognizing real alternatives available to the individual. The lack of involvement with our work expresses itself in the social sphere as a lack of involvement with each other. The result is loneliness. The depersonalization of work and the resulting alienation of the individual in modern, industrial society is surely one of the most troubling problems of our age.

The Jewish Talmud admonishes every intellectual and scholar to take up a trade or mechanical art.[5] The purpose of this is twofold: We should not depend on others for our physical sustenance, and physical labor provides a good counterdose to the exertion of the mind. The need for a balance between physical and mental activity has been part of the Jewish tradition from its earliest beginnings. Spinoza followed this noble admonition. He practiced the art of grinding lenses as a means for the satisfaction of his modest material needs, and he combined it with his scientific interest in the fast developing science of Optics. Unfortunately, the dust from the lens grinding has probably contributed to his consumptive illness and thereby hastened his premature death.

The German philosopher, Kuno Fischer, summarizes Spinoza's life as follows:

"The whole work of Spinoza's life was directed to one point: he sought to free himself from self deception, and its delusions. It was his deepest personal necessity. He perceived that the root of self deception is selfishness, which creates the tribe of our appetites, wishes and passions. As long as our mind is blinded by them, it is quite incapable of recognizing the truth. If we call love the opposite of selfishness, then the love of truth was the one ruling and enlightening motive in his life and character. His whole existence was a self renunciation for the sake of this love."[6]

For Spinoza, the essence of our existence was to say, yes to life. Only life enhancing and joyful patterns of existence are compatible with our true essence. Appearances are meant for the other, the essence is for oneself. Appearances complicate life, the essence simplifies it. Spinoza denied the freedom of the will but believed in the power of the individual to do away with any moribund and self-defeating tendencies, and to assert the joy of life over the irrational forces that bring about sadness, sorrow, and self-destruction.

Spinoza does not set a time frame for the process of self- mastery. No time limit exists for the need of an objective assessment of our life's essence. The possibilities for establishing personal harmony with our life's essence exist throughout our life time. "It is never to early or too late to occupy oneself with one's soul."[7] At whatever stage in life we realize our essence and the need to uphold its integrity rather than compromise it, we can achieve freedom, wholeness, and enlightenment. The refusal to compromise our life's essence and to maintain self-integrity regardless of all the odds against it, brings inner joy, serenity, strength, and happiness to the person. The ability to view ourselves and our life's essence (the essence of our existence) realistically, in the light of reason and truth, rather than through suppressed phantasy, brings with it the condition of self-fulfillment and the power to realize it. Past failure, evaluated with objective awareness turns into past experience and becomes a source of new understanding and new learning. And so, we may say with Kierkegaard, "life has to be understood backwards and lived forwards." Similarly, the ancient Hebrew sages have said "to sin is to miss the road. To miss and come back is better than not to have sinned at all." The road toward our true being is to recognize the reality of our situation, to follow the path of reason and enjoy the truth that reveals itself to us. This is the true sense of the idea of truth as discovery or unconcealment. We discover the truth that lies hidden within each of us. This self-discovery enhances our power to be and to live in joy. This is what Spinoza upheld in all of his teachings.

4. The Question of Character

"meanwhile man conceives a human character much more stable than his own, and he sees that there is no reason why he should not himself acquire such a character."[8] Similarly, Epictetus in "On the Finery in Dress," says: "it is character which makes a man beautiful."[9]

The stability and firmness of character is the very basis of our happiness. Spinoza's counsel "to acquire a character much more stable than his own" does not mean that we can at will change our character. We can acquire greater firmness of character by our enduring effort to understand ourselves. It will lead to greater self-mastery through self-knowledge.

What does knowing ourselves mean? For the Stoics, it meant to know our faults. We read in Seneca: "Will you not rather look at your own faults?"[10] In the *Philebus*, Plato defines ignorance of self as an overestimate of our wealth, appearance, or character. For Socrates, to know ourselves is to know the limits of our ability and character, namely, "to know the limits of one's wisdom." Self-knowledge must include knowledge of its limits.[11] We usually are prone to see the faults of others rather than ours. I am reminded of Aesop's fable of the two sacks that each of us carries. One is filled with our faults and the other with the faults of others. The one with our faults, we carry in the back, while the one with the others' faults, we carry in front.[12] Plotinus saw intellectual self-knowledge as "the turning of the mind upon itself until thinker and thought are one."[13] Philo Judaeus links self knowledge to Being "he who apprehends himself will, by clearly grasping the universal nothingness of creature...learn to know Being."[14]

Hence, self-determination requires self-knowledge. In order to make use of our strength, we have to overcome our weaknesses. Strength and weakness refer to character, knowledge, interests, motivations, values, beliefs, and goals. We learn about ourselves by objectively reflecting on our actions and experiences. Since we are more prone to see faults in others than in ourselves, self-discovery is greatly facilitated by self-exposure and by listening to what others are saying about us. Philo of Alexandria emphasizes listening to the truth without and within. He describes banquets of listening in which the people perfected the art of listening.[15]

The purpose of self-knowledge is to be in touch with ourselves in order to accept ourselves. As this takes place, we become more reality centered. We thereby ease our fears and anxieties. We come to rely more on our judgment and less on the judgment of others. We gain confidence in ourselves and we become more self-determined. We develop an awareness of the eternal and the spiritual within us. We realize that the spiritual part of our being gives meaning to our existence. We learn to cultivate inner peace and avoid mental chaos. Our mind becomes more lucid, our disposition more noble, and our body more poised. As we develop greater integrity of character, we become more humble. We don't feel the need to boast or impress others. We gain a sense of direction.

We understand that our environment at home or at work will never be ideal. We know that it is not structured to please or accommodate any one person. We learn to function optimally in a less than optimum environment. We become more mature. Learning to cope with reality is the essence of maturity. A mature person actively participates in the making of his or her surroundings. The person is shaped by it, but he or she also affects it and influences it. Only by living in reality can we change reality.

A realistic appreciation of our life's situation requires the fundamental recognition that we can only start from where we are now, and that we cannot recreate yesterday. We can change (improve) our understanding of the past, but we cannot make it undone. That is why Spinoza disparaged repentance and regret. "Repentance is not a virtue, that is to say, it does not spring from reason; on the contrary, the man who repents of what he has done is doubly wretched or impotent" (EIV, 54,).

Only by living in reality, that is, in accord with reason, can we realize our essence and our dreams. Real life and real living is always exhilarating. To live in reality is not to be swayed by exaggerated needs and dependencies. It avoids the double traps of delusion of grandeur and self-defeatism. Both of these share a common root in the person's infirmity of character. We must not give in to our physical and emotional losses that tax our hope, courage, vitality, and spirit.

Through the practice of self-discipline based on reason, through the conquest of unreason through understanding, we can neutralize adverse external conditions and turn them around to our advantage. The most adverse external conditions are those of personal isolation. We experience neither love nor friendship. Yet we can reconnect, if we can steady our character through disciplined self understanding. In this, Spinoza has a great deal to teach us. He is a shining beacon of light and an inspiration to all real seekers of wisdom, truth, and the meaning of our being.

Spinoza's character was pristinely pure and firm. The love of truth was his ruling passion and on it he would never compromise. No trace of vanity occurred in his character. He attached little importance to being praised or recognized by others for his exceptional intellect. Even his beloved teacher, who later turned against him, "was not well informed about the firmness of his mind." He thought that Spinoza would repent and avoid the coming punishment.[16]

The severe punishment of excommunication only strengthened young Spinoza's resolve to search for truth regardless of any consequences. He refused to depend on any one for his needs. In order to safeguard his independence, he chose to keep his needs to a bare but sufficient minimum. He chose to grind lenses for his daily bread, and refused to accept a professorship at Heidelberg in order not to compromise his freedom, even in the slightest degree. As a lens grinder, he very much excelled in his trade. "There is reason to believe that, if death had not prevented it, he would have discovered the most beautiful secrets of Optics."[17]

Spinoza was completely devoid of any affectation. Before his death, he instructed his landlord to submit his *Ethics* to the printer without his name on it, "saying that such affectations are not worthy of a philosopher."[18]

His earliest biographer, Lucas, who knew him well, makes the following comment on his external appearence: "He was extremely tidy in his clothes, without being pedantic."[19] Spinoza felt that a neglect of our appearance is the mark of an inferior character. He was not tempted by riches, and he had no fear of poverty. He was always ready to lend a helping hand to someone in need. For most of his life however, he was not in good health. And, "if he was susceptible to any sorrow, it was for the sorrow of others."[20] Spinoza was not an ascetic. He would enjoy simple pleasures, never allowing them to disturb "the tranquility of his soul."[21] In the knowledge of God "one finds perfect tranquility of spirit and the true love of God that brings us salvation, which is Blessedness and Freedom."[22] Ultimately, in the rejoicing of the knowledge of God (in the unity of the mind with the whole of nature) we become free from all negative and self-inhibiting emotions. The strength of this joy overcomes all opposite emotions.

Notes

1. Sigmund Freud, A Difficulty in the Path of Psychoanalysis, Standard Edition, vol.17, pp.137-144. *The Complete Psychological Works of Sigmund Freud*, Translated and edited by James Strachey, 24 vols. London: Hogarth Press, 1955.

2. Benedict De Spinoza, *On the Improvement of the Understanding*, Elwes Transl. New York: Dover Publications, Inc. 1955, p.6.

3. Ibid.

4. Plutarch: "One must direct one's efforts to the one pursuit to which one is naturally fitted and not spend one's life in imitation of others and do violence to one's nature", cited in : Elizabeth Gregory Wilkins,*"Know Thyself" in Greek and Latin Literature:* New York: Garland Pub.1917, p.2.

5. Kuno, Fischer, The Life and Character of Baruch Spinoza , in *Spinoza, Four Essays*, edited by W. Knight. London and Edinburgh: Williams and Northgate, 1882. pp.82-83.

6. Wilkins, ibid., p. 18.

7. Ibid.

8. Spinoza, ibid., p.6.

9. Wilkins, ibid., p.67.

10. Ibid., p.48.

11. Drew Hyland, *The Virtue of Philosophy: An Interpretation of Plato's Charmides*, Athens Ohio: Ohio university Press, 1981. p.103.

12. Wilkins, ibid., p.41.

13. Ibid., p.49.

14. Ibid., pp.71-72.

15. Ibid., p.81.

16. A. Wolf, ed. *The Oldest Biography of Spinoza*. London: George Allen & Unwin Ltd., 1927. p.50.

17. Ibid., p.60.

18. Ibid., p.62.

19. Ibid., p. 62.

20. Ibid., p.65.

21. Ibid., pp. 68-69

22. Ibid., p.70.

CHAPTER 5
THE NATURE OF HUMAN EMOTIONS AND THE CONCOMITANT JOY OF TRUE COGNITION

1. The Control of Emotions qua Emotions

One of Spinoza's most fundamental insights into the nature of human emotions, is that an emotion can only be destroyed by a contrary and stronger emotion. "An emotion can only be controlled or destroyed by another emotion contrary thereto, and with more power for controlling emotion" (EIV, 7).

In the preface to part 5 of the Ethics, Spinoza says that he will show the dominion of the mind over the emotions, namely, "how far the reason can control the emotions", or "the power of the reason" to control the emotions. The question that needs to be asked is this: If an emotion can only be destroyed or controlled by another emotion, by what mechanism does the mind control an emotion? What is the bridge between an emotion or passion and the mind's possible control over it? Is cognition itself an emotion?

The question has escaped most of Spinoza's commentators, except for Stuart Hampshire, who touches on this question in a marginal way.[1] Since the question was not posed (at least not explicitly), no formal answer could have been given to it.

The proposition that emotions can only be dealt with qua emotions (EIV, 7) certainly agrees with our experience. An emotional loss will be quickly overcome by an emotional gain. Life provides ample evidence of that. Arguably, this proposition together with psycho-physical parallelism (EII, 7) form the core of the whole of Spinoza's Ethics, namely, the idea of freedom. The psychophysical theorem pertains to our understanding of God, and (IV, 7) deals with our liberation from passions, without which we could neither come to know God, nor ourselves.

In what follows, I work out an answer to the question posed. Before doing that, let us reformulate the question: How to reconcile the mind's control over the emotions with the proposition that emotions can only be controlled qua emotions. Let us proceed with the answer:

1. Spinoza defines an emotion as "the modification of the body, whereby its active power is increased or diminished together with the idea of such modification" (EIII, Def.3). An emotion always involves the body and the mind (idea of body) and the concurrent positive or negative change in their corresponding powers to act and to think.

2. An emotion that is a passion is based on an inadequate or confused idea (EIII, 3), "But in so far as the mind has inadequate ideas, it is necessarily passive" (EIII, 3, Schol.). The cause of the passion is always an external one. It is based on imagination rather than on truth. All emotions that involve pain (all negative emotions) are brought about by external causes, whereby the mind is passive and it has confused ideas about them.

3. A passion, by its nature, dominates us to the extent that we are wholly involved in it and cannot separate ourselves from it. We cannot separate our mind from the external causes that we perceive confusedly.

4. Once we correctly understand the nature of the passion, we put in distance between ourselves and the emotion. Without distancing ourselves from the emotion, we cannot understand it. This is clearly stated in EV, 3: "An emotion which is a passion, ceases to be a passion, as soon as we form a clear and distinct idea thereof." In our understanding of the passion (in our distancing ourselves from it and in our forming a clear and distinct idea of it), the passion loses its grip over us and we are no more controlled or dominated by it.

5. Next, we must understand the nature of the external cause (or causes) of the passion. For, "there is no modification of the body whereof we cannot form some clear and distinct conception" (EV, 4). And, "everyone has the power of clearly and distinctly understanding himself and his emotions..." (EV, 4, Note). Most commentators, among them, Jon Wetlesen,[2] Arne Naess,[3] Thomas Carson Mark,[4] in their discussion of the connection between cognition and emotion stop more or less here. They don't go beyond the point whereby the mind realizes that the external causes of the passion consist primarily of the mind's own projections, and

that these may be understood "through their immanent and adequate causes and thereby cognized adequately."[5] Wetlesen makes an unjustified leap by linking the understanding of a given passion with the need to understand all passions and God, " in seeing all modes as the effects of the immanent causality of God". And ..."when a passion has attained this degree of self knowledge, his faculty of imagination is free...and he depends on his own nature alone." [6]

By connecting the understanding of a particular passion with the freedom from all passions, Wetlesen unnecessarily complicates the problem of the mind's power over the passions. It becomes difficult for the mind to deal with anyone passion. Wetlesen does not consider the last point, since he combines it with total freedom and the intellectual love of God *(amor dei intellectualis)*. While it is not inconceivable that one may attain instantaneous or sudden liberation, the freedom from all passions is not a necessary or concurrent condition for Spinoza's view of the mind's ability to control the emotions. Instead, Spinoza unfolds a gradualist approach to human freedom and the mind's control over the emotions.

Naess correctly singles out the connection between emotion and power, but he reverses the true order of causation. The road to freedom is "through the activation of emotion." The more active, intense, and persistent the emotions, the more rapid the transition to higher levels of freedom. An increase in power is simultaneously an increase in freedom. Naess reasons from the intensity of the active emotion to "being in oneself" to being "the adequate cause of one's action" and "to self-understanding."[7] Naess reverses the process of the dominion of the mind over the emotions. If an emotion can only be destroyed by a contrary emotion that is more intense than itself, the intensity of the passion will increase our bondage to it, unless it is overcome by a stronger, more intense emotion. Whence comes this activation of the emotion? Naess does not spell this out. He does not clarify the link between the mind's dominion over the emotions and the overcoming of negative emotions by positive ones.

6. We need to establish the links in the process of freedom from passions qua passions. When the mind has a clear and distinct idea of the nature of the passion and of its external cause, the mind is necessarily active (EIII, 1). Every increase in the activity of the mind increases its power to form adequate ideas, the mind's power of understanding. Since, "the more things the mind knows, the better it understands its own

strength and the order of nature: by increased self knowledge, it can direct itself more easily..." (*On the Improvement of the Understanding*, Elwes Transl. p.15). The enhanced power of the mind increases its independence or self-dependence. The mind is less subject to imagination and to having inadequate ideas of external causes. This makes us more self-determined and thereby enhances our real freedom.

7. Now comes the most important link in the chain of causation: Every increase in real freedom (active self- determination and self-direction, an increase in virtue, power, and reality) is necessarily and always accompanied by a feeling of joy. A feeling of joy accompanies every increase in the understanding of the truth of our being. The enhanced self-knowledge and truth increases our power of self-direction. This is the internal source and cause of the joyful feeling. It depends wholly on my increased understanding of myself and not on any outside cause. The joy associated with the activity of the mind (an active emotion) is necessarily stronger than the passive and negative emotion of pain that it replaces. The emotion of joy brought about by the enhanced freedom of the mind through understanding will necessarily conquer and destroy the passive emotion of pain, which is based on a confused and inadequate idea of itself and its external cause. The action of the mind is directly proportional to the intensity of the passion, and in every case will the joy be greater than the pain being replaced by it. This is how the mind through understanding, can control the bodily passions. Most commentators have failed to point out this connecting link in the chain of causation.

8. Now, we must issue a caveat: Only a true understanding enhances our freedom. A quasi or deceptive understanding (self-deception) will never do it. Since most people are not readily capable of forming a true understanding of their passions, their mind's ability to control the emotions is limited, at best. Some emotions may be subject to many external causes, both conscious and unconscious. People may have long-standing inclinations towards certain kinds of negative emotions (personality or character traits). These may be much more difficult to know and deal with internally than the more simple emotions. Similarly, some of the confused and inadequate ideas (external causes of negative emotions) may have been with us for a long time, while others may have been of short duration. The former will be much more difficult to deal with than the latter. Any combination of these and kindred factors may operate behind our compound and complex emotions. How to sift them out will

present a real challenge to anyone's mind in its effort to understand itself and become more free.

2. The Conquest of Passion

The conquest of each passion brings us a step closer to our ability to activate our mind and thereby to determine ourselves from within. In each self-activation, we are the cause of the ideas of ourselves (*ideae ideaerum* or self-conscious ideas, whereby the first idea of the modification of the body is the *ideatum* for the other idea, and thereby idea and *ideatum* perfectly correspond to each other). When our mind is self- active, our ideas are self-generated or *causa sui*. Our mind being part of nature and underlying all the natural laws, partakes in its ability to understand itself and God, in the divine principle of *natura naturans*, which constitute its link to nature's self creation (*causa sui*).

And so we may establish that the bridge betweeen the passion and the understanding, that goes through an enhancement of real freedom and is accompanied by a feeling of joy, is also a bridge that connects the individual to God. This is how we participate in the divine creation.

To the extent that we act in accordance with our nature, that is, to the extent that we determine ourselves, we are like God. We create and recreate ourselves (in the world of ideas through the divine attribute of thought) by self-causation (*causa sui*) and the eternally active, powerful, and dynamic principle of *Natura naturans*. To the extent that we are passive and determined, we remain forever a mode (*Natura naturata*). In freedom, we can continuously change the proportion of *Natura naturans* and *Natura naturata*, the creative and the created principles of nature, that reside within us. ("God is in man"). We can increase the one at the expense of the other.

In the process of becoming free from the passions, we are involved in the transition from confused and inadequate ideas to clear and distinct ideas about the nature and the cause of the passion. It is a transition from imagination to reason (*imaginatio* to *ratio*), from the first to the second kind of knowledge. The joy that overpowers the negative emotion comes from the enhanced freedom gained by the increase in self-understanding. Every true self-cognition brings with it a greater sense of real freedom and this evokes in us a feeling of joy.

Can we now turn the argument around and state that whenever an insight into ourselves is accompanied by a feeling of joy, it will necessarily be a true insight? Can we generalize this to hold for any true cognition? Can we say, that joy is a measure of truth? I argue that for Spinoza this is the case.

The process of the freeing of ourselves from the passions is still bound up with objective or representational thinking. The passion is always based on a confusion of thought, on a mixture of distinct and indistinct, adequate and inadequate ideas. In working out the confusion, we separate the clear and distinct ideas and free them from their entanglement with the confused ideas. Through our understanding of the passion, that is, through application of reason (common notions that are equally in part and in the whole, EII, 38) to the emotion, our mind is active. The newly discovered truth pertains to the nature and to the external cause of the passion. The enhanced freedom evokes joy. The joy is a consequence of self-truth.

This feeling of joy is intensified in the transition from representational and object-oriented cognition to the intuitive and subject-centered truth, from the second to the third kind of knowing. Intuitive truth opens itself up to us in a flash of discovery. The newly conceived insight is not any more a last link in a deductive chain of reasoning. It is an instantaneous comprehension of a totality. It is like all the links in the long process of representational (scientific) thinking compressed into one. The mind comes to comprehend Being or Substance itself, an immediate unity of the mind with the whole of nature. We have come to grasp God in ourselves.

The joy of this total immersion in truth by far exceeds any empirical joy resulting from the partial liberation from any given passion. The joy itself has become spiritualized. We have entered a state of blessedness. To grasp God in ourselves is the same as the intellectual love of God (*amor dei intellectualis*). The distinctions betwen the self and the not-self, subject and object, truth and freedom have vanished. We have come to be connected to the Absolute. The state of blessedness is the spiritual joy of this connection to freedom.

3. The Connection between Truth and Freedom

The connection between truth and freedom is fundamental. The idea of freedom for Spinoza, is ontologically more fundamental than Being.

Being could not be without a free cause *(causa sui)*. In the universe of finite modes, the universal endeavor of each thing to self-preserve, that is, its *conatus*, is itself an expression of each mode's striving to persist in freedom.

For Spinoza, a free thing acts from the necessity of its nature. It is not compelled to act by an external cause. In other words, the cause of action (existence) of a free thing is within it, not outside it (EI, Def.7). We, as modes of Extension or physical bodies, can never be free in this sense. Only God is free in all of His attributes. As physical beings, we can never be free, because, "every individual thing or everything which is finite and has a conditioned existence, cannot exist or be conditioned to act, unless it be conditioned for existence and action by a cause other than itself, which is also finite, and has a conditioned existence; and likewise this cause cannot in its turn exist, or be conditioned to act, unless it be conditioned for existence and action by another cause, which also is finite, and has a conditioned existence, and so on to infinity" (EI. 28). Only nature as a whole is entirely determined by itself alone (EI, Def.7). The whole of nature (God) cannot have a cause, because that cause would itself be included in the whole of nature. Therefore, the whole of nature (God) is self-caused.

We, as finite modes, can never be free as physical beings (modifications under God's attribute of Extension). We can be free however as thinking beings (as modifications under God's attribute of Thought). We are free to the extent that we have true ideas. The truth of our ideas must come from reflective knowledge *(ideae idearum)*. It is a reflective truth. It cannot be based on imagination or images of external objects. Our image of a physical body will by necessity be distorted since it is based on a partial view of the real thing. We can never through our senses gain access to the totality (the thing in itself) of anything. In sensory cognition, there can never be a complete correspondence between the idea and the *ideatum*, or the idea and the physical object. Only in God is such correspondence total, complete, and absolute (EII, 7). We cannot achieve adequate truth, or correspondence between *essentia formalis*, (the thing in itself), and *essentia objectiva* (which Elwes translates as the subjective essence of the things), on the level of sensory perception. However, as reflective knowledge, in the realm of ideas of ideas, or when the initial ideas are the ideata of subsequent ideas and the latter become the ideata of further ideas, etc., may truth as correspondence between idea and *ideatum* prevail.

Our mind can form adequate ideas about itself and the universe (God). In self-reflection, in the understanding of ourselves and of our ideas about ourselves, our mind can be free. To the extent that we do this, we are free. As finite modes, human beings can only be free and self determined in the realm of the intellect. That is, as a mode in Thought, we can have true ideas.

When we have true ideas, we are the cause of our action. We are the cause of our ideas when we act from understanding. Whenever we act from understanding, our action is a free action. Thus, we come close to Substance itself. Since understanding always means acting from reason, or acting in accordance with the dictates of reason, it is the same as true knowing. Therefore, every free act is based on true knowing. Without true knowing, it could not be a free act. This establishes the necesssary unity of truth and freedom.

Since freedom is always accompanied by a feeling of joy, there is an identical and necessary corresponding connection between truth and joy. And, since the highest expression of this truth (the truth of our ideas about ourselves and the world) comes through our intuition (the third kind of knowing), we can take the joy that is connected with it, as a measure of truth. The intensity of this joy will simultaneously be a measure of the depth of our truth. The depth of this truth will be revealed to us when the mind grasps the essence of Substance. Such truth is available to us. "The human mind possesses an adequate knowledge of the eternal and infinite essence of God" (EII, 47). When we grasp this truth, we will know that we have grasped it. We do not need any Cartesian meditation to know it. "He who has a true idea, simultaneously knows that he has a true idea, and cannot doubt of the truth of the thing perceived" (EII, 43). For Spinoza, the adequacy of an idea follows from its internal properties alone. The true idea represents and is part of the order and connection of things, in the Attribute of Thought.

When the mind grasps the truth, its power of acting is always increased. Since the cause of the action is internal (in the mind having adequate ideas), such action is necessarily a free act *(causa sui)*. Truth and freedom are for Spinoza dynamic principles that emanate in the free actions of the mind. Every free act is an act in truth. And every understanding of the truth is a free act. Every time we grasp a true idea, or whenever we comprehend the truth, we become more free. This freedom gives us pleasure. Every free act is a joyful act. It is not possible to dissassociate pleasure from freedom.

4. The Progression in the Realm of Cognition

The progression in the realm of cognition, from *imaginatio* to *ratio* to *scientia intuitiva* is also a progression in the realm of emotion from confusion (pain) to pleasure (truth) to spiritual joy (blessedness). Thinking reaches its highest stage in intuition. Intuitive thinking cannot be in opposition to scientific or perceptual thinking. There is truth also in *imaginatio* or image thinking. In this lowest level of knowing, our ideas are confused, because adequate and inadequate ideas are mixed together. When representational thinking based on the level of sensual perception becomes purified by *ratio* (reason), it reaches the level of science (adequate ideas). There is however another kind of imagination that is based purely on the intellect, not on the senses. This intuitive and non-representational thinking corresponds to Spinoza's third level of knowing. Through creative imagination we penetrate the hidden layers of things. In between sensual perception and intuition lies *ratio*, which is at the base of scientific thinking.

Science can only deal with segments or parts of reality. It captures them in their static state. Scientific thinking (quantification and measurement), analyzes parts of the real world in their fixity. Science can never catch the durational flow itself. Scientific or analytic thinking can only look at the thing from the outside in order to ascertain its essential qualities. Not even the most powerful scientific instrument can change this fact. They still measure reality from the outside of the thing, namely through observation. No scientific instrument can put itself inside the thing and get a view of it from there, to see how it is from the inside looking out. This can only be accomplished through the creative imagination and intuition. Intuition does what science cannot do. It completes the work of science. Only through intuition can we place ourselves inside a blade of grass (to use the Kantian metaphor in the Third Critique), inside a tree, a bird, or you and me. There is no need to stop the durational flow of the parts of the thing to dissect and analyze them. In intuition, we can capture being in becoming and becoming in being. We can see the whole in the part and the part in the whole. We can grasp God and the whole of nature. Intuitive thinking is free, creative and does not depend on representations. We have freed ourselves from the strict rules of scientific and analytical thinking. Witness the meaning and affinity of the words, (insight) and (intuition). Insight means a seeing from within, and intuition means a learning from within. Only with our intellect can we grasp the nature of the thing in itself, the core of the real. Only through intuition can we shift our perspective from the outside of the thing to the inside of the thing. What intuition grasps will eventually have to be subjected to scientific scrutiny for its objective verification or refutation. In all science, theoretical and practical knowledge, representational and non-representational or intuitive thinking complement each other. Metaphysics complements and guides physics. (Aristotelian *Metaphysica* means after physics in the sense that metaphysical knowledge comes after physical knowledge.) Every scientific hypothesis rests initially on intuition. All advances in the sciences have initially been in the form of an intuitive hypotheses that later became part of the cumulative fund of general knowledge.

Intuition complements and fulfills scientific thinking. A direct correlation exists between perceptive understanding, (integration of perceptions and the depth of scientific knowledge), and the ability for intuitive penetration into the unknown. "The more we understand particular things, the more we understand God" (EV, 24). Intuitive thinking is personal and subjective. Understanding and internalization or integration of knowledge are its essential preconditions. No absolute break between perception and intuition, between physics and metaphysics exists. The visible and the invisible gradually reach and penetrate into each other. We commonly associate intuition with the arts and distinguish it from the sciences. There is however no clear break between the two. True science and true art, scientific and artistic vision ultimately merge together and become one in intuition.

Intuitive thinking is always accompanied by intense inner sensations and feelings. The intensity of the feelings will most likely be related to the intensity and complexity of the subject matter, as well as to the depth of the individual's involvement with it. The intensity of feeling and the joy of discovery will parallel the felt truth of the intuitive insight. Thus, joy becomes a measure of truth in intuition. Spinoza's state of blessedness is the affirmation of the highest intuitive penetration into the cosmic mystery and its revelation in knowledge. We capture God's eternity in His eternal presence, *"the third kind of knowledge is eternal"* (EV, 33, Schol.). Intuitive thinking and the third kind of knowledge "belongs to the essence of the mind and is necessarily eternal" (Ibid, demonst.). It is not in time. It is an eternal presence. In the penetration into the innermost layers of nature, into the inner nature of the thing (the thing in itself), the awareness of time ceases to exist. The concentration of the mind upon its thought is total. Thought and feeling, knower and known, merge into an identity and become indistinguishable from one another. This fusion of thought and feeling is the ultimate and highest expression of freedom. It is the state of blessedness itself, *amor dei intellectualis*.

5. Reality, Perfection and the Meaning of Good and Bad in Spinoza

Spinoza's concepts of good and bad are related to his notions of truth and freedom. Spinoza defines good as "that which we certainly know to be useful to us" (EV, Def.1). Evil is defined as "that which we certainly know to be a hindrance to us in the attainment of any good" (EIV, Def.2). Good or bad depends on whether we are hindered or helped in becoming free. That is, whatever increases our power of free action (our power of self-determination) is certainly useful to us. What diminishes that power is detrimental to our well-being. By power, Spinoza always means the power of the mind to understand the nature of things. It can never be physical power, because as a mode in the attribute of Extension, we can never be free. Our freedom lies in the truth of our understanding, that is, in our following the dictates of reason.

Power, for Spinoza is not the power that flows from the barrel of a gun (the Maoist concept of freedom), nor is it the power that flows from the accumulation of wealth or money power (the capitalist concept of freedom). Money, to the extent that it serves as an end rather than a means, may turn into evil, since it in fact curtails our inner freedom of self-determination, (to act from within and to be a free cause of our actions). Hence, both the utilitarian approach to self interest or usefulness (exemplified in Jeremy Bentham's philosophy which posits the supreme ethical principle as the greatest happiness of the greatest number,[8] as well as William James' pragmatic approach to truth (the truth of a concept lies in its practical consequences and uses),[9] are in opposition to Spinoza's meaning of the terms good and bad as useful or useless. Useful, for Spinoza is what enhances our true freedom. Evil is what prevents our freedom. Good and bad have cognitive (truth and untruth) as well as emotional content (freedom and bondage). Good in this sense is derivative of freedom. Freedom is the foundational idea from which the idea of good is derived.

Our highest freedom is not a freedom that we acquire in order to rule and subject nature. Neither is it a freedom to subject and rule over other people. Freedom, for Spinoza, is our power to understand God and thereby partake in the divine power of self-creation *(causa sui)*. When we use our creative powers, we act in freedom. This acting in freedom is our happiness. Aristotle defines happiness as "an activity *(energeia)* of the soul in accordance with perfect virtue" *(Nichomachean Ethics*, 1102 b 5). For Aristotle, "happiness...is something final and self sufficient, and it is the end of action" (ibid., 1097, b 22). Happiness is the final end, the highest good, and the most sufficient one.

For Spinoza, however, happiness is not a final end or the highest good. There is no *summum bonum* for which we strive as final end. Happiness or the good, is for Spinoza, our striving to self-preserve and be free, (to follow the dictates of reason). Happiness is not a reward for virtue, but virtue is its own reward. Thus, "Blessedness is not the reward of virtue, but virtue itself" (EV, 42). And, "He, who loves God, cannot endeavor that God should love him in return" (EV,19).

Some commentators[10] have assigned an indirect final end to Spinoza, and thus they identify him too closely with Aristotle. Bidney bases this on EV, 39, Schol., where Spinoza speaks "of the individual as subject to continuous change, 'for the better or the worse'. This, according to Bidney, involves an implicit final cause, "since the qualities of better and worse have no meaning except as approximations to a given ideal or goal."[11] He states, "contrary to Spinoza's conclusion that self-preservation is identical with virtue and happiness (EIV, 18, Schol.), we now find that self-preservation is only a condition of human happiness but is not identical with the latter."[12] Unfortunately, Bidney renders a superficial interpretation of Spinoza's *conatus* or desire for self-preservation. He excludes self-elevation from self-preservation, whereby EV, 39, Schol. specifically makes self-elevation inclusive in self-preservation. "In this life....we primarily endeavor to bring it about, that the body of a child....may be changed into something else capable of very many activities, and referrable to a mind which is highly conscious of itself, of God and of things" (EV, 39, Schol.).

The question of happiness as a final end (Aristotle) or as a consequence (a by product) of virtue (*conatus* or power) is a fundamental question that sets Spinoza apart from Aristotle. For Spinoza, we don't live in order to be happy. We are happy if we live as free human beings under the guidance of reason. The free person does not strive for the good, but the good is in the striving itself. This also differentiates Spinoza from Epicurus and his followers who saw in pleasure or the good a final cause of desire.

Our interest lies in "our faculty for existing and enjoying the rational life" (EIV, 7, App.). What promotes this, also promotes our power of free acting and understanding, which is good. Whatever hinders it, is bad. Thus,"in no case do we strive for, wish for, long for or desire anything, because we deem it to be good, but ....we deem a thing to be good because we strive for it, wish for it, long for it or desire it" (EIII, 9, Note). Good is what enhances our self-preservation and our self-elevation. What is detrimental to this is bad.

Notes

1. Stuart Hampshire, *Spinoza and the Idea of Freedom*, in Studies in Spinoza, S. Paul Kashap, ed. pp. 310-331.
2. Jon Wetlesen, *The Sage and the Way*, Assen, Netherlands: Van Gorcum, 1979, p. 284.
3. Arne Naess, *Freedom, Emotion and Self Substance,: The Structure of a Central Part of Spinoza's Ethics*, Oslo: Universitetsvorlaget, 1975, p. 83.
4. Thomas Carson Mark, *Spinoza's Theory of Truth* , New York: Columbia University Press, 1972, p.108.
5. Ibid.
6. Wetlesen, ibid. p.285.
7. Naess, ibid. 83.
8. J.S. Mill and Jeremy, Bentham, *Utalitarianism and Other Essays*. ed. Alan Ryan. New York: Penguin Books, 1987.

76

9.   Admittedly, this is a narrow interpretation of pragmatism. See, William James, *Pragmatism; A New Name for Some Old Ways of Thinking*. Indianapolis: Hackett Pub. Co., 1981.

10.   David Bidney, *The Psychology and Ethics of Spinoza*, New York: Russell and Russell, 1962, p.342.

11.   Ibid.

12.   Ibid.

CHAPTER 6
SELF-KNOWLEDGE THROUGH
INTROSPECTION AND SELF-UNDERSTANDING

Unexposed unconscious drives and irrational impulses detrimentally affect our conscious behavior. They make us act self-destructively. We are not aware of these unconscious impulses when they influence or determine our conscious actions. Through introspection and self-analysis we can expose unconscious drives, become aware of them, and neutralize their paralyzing effect on us. We can free ourselves from our fixations through the understanding of their true nature. "Human infirmity in moderating and checking the emotions I name bondage: for, when a man is prey to his emotions, he is not his own master, but lies at the mercy of fortune: so much so, that he is often compelled, while seeing that which is better for him, to follow that which is worse" (EIV, Preface). Our purpose in this chapter is to inquire into the nature of our basic, inner conflicts that stand in the way of our understanding of ourselves, and of our living a full and joyful life. Self-understanding extends itself also to the understanding of the objective conditions of our existence.

I. INNER CONFLICT

1. The Origin of Internal Conflict

An internal conflict pertains to our inability to accept some aspect of our real self. We tend to substitute an imaginary part of the self for the real self. We are thus unable to see ourselves objectively, and accept ourselves unconditionally. Therein lies the essence of our basic inner conflict. The particular form and manifestation of the conflict will differ between people. The manifestations of the conflict are specific to the individual, since they are shaped by the circumstances of the person's life. The origin of the basic conflict can usually be traced to infancy or early childhood experiences. We carry over and internalize our parents' conflicts, their unexpressed ambitions and unfulfilled expectations. The parental conflict is transmitted to the infant non-verbally in the form of heightened anxiety, inconsistent attitudes, erratic and unreliable behavior, recurrent depression, selfishness, self-preoccupation, and a lack of patience. The child thinks of itself as being the cause of the parental anxiety, and feels rejected. It compensates for this by forming a perfectionist, imaginary self by which it hopes to gain the parents' love. This is the root cause of the basic, internal conflict.

The basic conflict will evolve into a number of secondary conflicts which rigidify the person's behavior over time. Any unresolved derivative conflict may stabilize into rigid reaction patterns in the body, in the form of muscular tension, and rigid thought and behavior patterns in the mind. Reactions in body and mind proceed simultaneously. Once a particular conflict has stabilized into a definite reaction pattern, it will tend to persist. The person's reaction to certain stimuli will be predetermined, and fixed. The person will act compulsively.

Body and mind are perfectly equivalent to each other. "Body cannot determine mind to think, neither can mind determine body to motion or rest or any state different from these, if such there be" (EIII, 2). "Mind and body are one and the same thing, conceived first under the attribute of thought, secondly, under the attribute of extension" (Ibid. Note). The unity of body and mind is at the base of the meditation and relaxation techniques both in the East and in the West.[1] The mind-body unity means that every single thought throughout our whole life had its exact counterpart in the body, and correspondingly, every affection of the body that we have ever experienced in our life, from infancy to the present, had its exact counterpart in the mind. Let us take, for example, pain and pleasure as expressed in body and mind. A painful thought expresses stress (uneasiness and lack of peace) in the mind, and tension in the body. Bodily tension and mental stress are equivalent and identical with each other. A joyful thought expresses calmness and mental peace in the mind and relaxation in the body. Tension in the body expresses mental stress and body relaxation expresses mental calmness. We are usually aware of a distressing thought that we have in our mind, but we are not aware of its counterpart in the body, since it is so minimal as to make it impossible to detect. Nevertheless, the bodily counterpart of each thought is always there. This means that all our thoughts throughout our entire life time have had their simultaneous expressions in our body. The same holds for all our bodily affections and their counterparts in our mind. While the bodily counterpart of each thought is not visible by itself, and cannot therefore be immediately detected, it is nevertheless cumulative and thus affects the condition of our body. The condition of our body becomes visible only after a protracted accumulation of painful or pleasurable thoughts. The way we live our life expresses itself through our body as well as through our mind. Pleasurable and life asserting thoughts relax and preserve the health of our body. Painful and distressing thoughts tense our muscles and make our body deteriorate. Thus, "Mirth cannot be excessive, but is always good; contrariwise, Melancholy is always bad" (EIV, 42). This is why some people age faster than others, and other people stay younger than others. When we exercise our body and mind we live longer and stay younger. When we spend our lives in poverty and squalor we get prematurely old. The exact parallelism of body and mind is easily seen in our facial expressions. Our face reflects the nature of our thoughts and feelings simultaneously. When we have pleasurable thoughts we have a happy face. When we have painful thoughts we have an unhappy face. We need to remember however, that our entire body (not only the face) registers, and expresses the nature of our thoughts and feelings. This is what directly links body and mind into the same unity. Mental calmness expresses unity and coherence of thought. Mental distress expresses thought fragmentation and conflict.

Calmness and stress in the mind are directly related to the way we deal with inner conflict. We are not normally aware of the conflict that operates beneath our compulsive behavior. We are not even aware that we act compulsively. Through introspection and self analysis we can become aware of our compulsions and bring them into the open. We can uncover the internal conflict that is behind our compulsive and fixed behavior patterns.

The inability of people to accept themselves as they are (the root cause of the basic conflict) goes back to the early home environment. The seeds for this conflict have been for the most part laid in infancy. The infant is entirely dependent on others (his parents). A child is born with avenues of potential development wide open. Inheritance determines rough outer limits of his potential growth in any direction. These limits are never fully reached in any one person's life time. Since actual development will always stop short of potential, it makes potential development of any human being practically limitless. ("No one knows the limits of the body or of the mind.") This means that any person has the ability to further develop his or her inner resources at all times. The resolution of inner conflict is a necessary precondition for the person's individual freedom, and optimum development.

Let us take an example: Suppose the person's basic conflict manifests itself in the need to be accomplished in everything he or she does. What is the root cause of this conflict? We know that the seeds of the conflict have been laid in infancy or early childhood. Experiences during infancy, however, are not available to us through memory. We can learn about them from those who took care of us, but such information will tend to be distorted. We are thus left with those childhood experiences that are stored in our conscious mind and can be recreated through memory. We may try to recollect when it was the first time that we have experienced internal conflict. We may recall that early in life we have developed the need to be admired by others and to be accomplished in whatever we do. The need for admiration inhibited the child's freeedom to act spontaneously. This may have led to exaggerated sensitivity, self-consciousness and shyness. Behind it was perhaps the mother's expectation of the child's future greatness which she communicated to the child in a variety of ways. The mother's love was not perceived by the child as unconditional and pure.

The general syndrome of shyness and heightened sensitivity hampered the free development of the child's faculties by preventing or interfering with its readiness to expose itself freely to unfamiliar situations and surroundings. The general syndrome embodied fear of exposure, inhibition, and excessive sensitivity to judgment. The result was a lack of self-confidence, and a persistent state of inner insecurity. The child's potential development has been stunted. As we grow up, we are semiaware of this conflict but are unable to deal with it on the conscious level. There is a tendency to suppress it rather than to deal with it.

2. The Nature of the Basic Conflict

In the example given above, the basic conflict pertains to the person's inability to accept his or her normal imperfections. This precludes the individual from developing self-confidence and self-trust. It makes the person excessively dependent on the judgment of others. The need for outside approval becomes exaggerated and it adversely affects the person's ability to make self-serving choices. The individual's development is slanted.

It is difficult to know exactly what early life experiences bring about the inability to accept ourselves for our own sake. We may speculate about some of the probable causes. These may include the following:

1. If during infancy the mother's love has come to be associated with praise for the child's exceptional qualities, it made the child connect love with perfection. If love had been conditioned by perfection, self consciousness will tend to develop. The child thinks subconsciously that in order to be loved, it must exhibit certain qualities worthy of admiration.

2. The child learns to anticipate the mother's expectations and acts accordingly. This reinforces the child's dependency needs and diminishes the ability to be self-dependent. Its self-confidence has been adversely affected.

3. Even if the mother's love for her child is pure and unconditional, the form in which this love expresses itself (excessive admiration and praise for some of the child's exceptional qualities) may lead to the forming of an association between love and perfection in the child's mind. A conflict may develop between the need for unconditional acceptance and the reality of love being conditioned by certain admirable qualities of behavior. This will lay the seeds of future conflict.

4. If love is associated with perfection, an inability to self- accept will develop. This will cause shyness, retreat, inhibition, and insecurity from an early age. Inhibition and the fear of exposure of one's imperfections will lead to an uneven development of the child's faculties. Faculties that need not be exposed may develop excessively, (mental activity and a tendency to become introverted), while those faculties that depend on risk taking or self-exposure (speech and social interactions) may not develop sufficiently, due to lack of practice.

5. The child would become excessively dependent on the judgment of others and would be afraid of being judged. The need for perfection will

become internalized and the child will feel ashamed when its imperfections are exposed. Since it is not possible to be perfect no matter how smart or intelligent we are, a generalized inability to accept ourselves will develop. Feelings of inferiority will result.

6. To compensate for inferiority feelings the child may protect itself by developing an exaggerated sense of its power or self-importance. This will lead to over-compensation, and heightened self-consciousness.

7. The enhanced sensitivity to other people's judgments will foster dependency patterns and a loss of inner freedom. It will crystalize into character weakness. Particular manifestations of the dependency syndrome may take a variety of forms, such as: doubt and vacillation of mind, a tendency to procrastinate, to be indecisive, and an inability to stay with a given decision or course of action. "This disposition of the mind, which arises from two contrary emotions, is called vacillation;....vacillation and doubt do not differ one from the other, except as greater differs from less" (EIII, 17, Note). The individual's behavior will appear inconsistent and conflicted. This will deny the person peace of mind. The person will seem tense, restless, and uneasy. A concurrent tendency to rationalize one's actions will evolve.

8. Decisions that are not freely made will bring about renewed inner conflict. Actions and decisions emanating from a generalized dependency syndrome will gradually evolve into fixed behavior patterns. Within such behavior responses, dependent choices become submerged under the guise of (apparent) free choice. Dependent and free choices become indistinguishable from each other. This is the more so, since all actions are made on a voluntary basis and therefore appear to the indidvidual as free choices. As this continues, the internal conflict that is inherent in the unfree choice will itself become suppressed. The person will no longer feel the pain or the awareness of his or her conflict. The internal conflict will no longer serve as a warning signal comparable to physical pain in the case of illness. A loss of mental agility and a greater loss of individual freedom will ensue.

9. The general syndrome of shyness, inhibition, self-consciousness, and exaggerated sensitivity will be accompanied by an acute feeling of shame. The shame results from the fear of violating some acculturated or paternally set norms of social behavior. The shame acts as an inhibitor of behavior that is not sanctioned by society, "shame, like compassion is not a virtue, is yet good, in so far as it shows, that the feeler of shame is really

imbued with the desire to live honourably;" (EIV, 58, Note.) Shame contains an element of guilt but it is much broder than guilt. A person may feel ashamed without feeling guilty. The individual may be ashamed of being singled out in a group for whatever reason. In this case, shame is more an aspect of shyness than guilt. The feeling of shame is associated with the fear of exposing certain personal defects or weaknesses. The most generalized aspect of shame is symbolized by the fear of being caught naked in public. Thus, "pleasure accompanied by the idea of an external cause we will style *Honour*, and the emotion contrary thereto we will style *Shame*: I mean in such cases as where pleasure or pain arises from a man's belief, that he is being praised or blamed:....Again, as it may happen that the pleasure, wherewith a man conceives that he affects others, may exist solely in his own imagination, and as everyone endeavours to conceive concerning himself that which he conceives will affect him with pleasure, it may easily come to pass that a vain man may be proud and may imagine that he is pleasing to all, when in reality he may be an annoyance to all." (EIII, 30, Note.) And, "an ambitious man desires nothing so much as glory, and fears nothing so much as shame" (EIII, 39, Note).

10. If we are overly sensitive to what other people say or think about us, we will be inhibited in our ability to impose our choices, desires or convictions on the environment. We will behave according to the presumed or anticipated norms of others rather than those of our own. The need to avoid negative judgment may become pervasive, and we will gradually become detached from reality. We may create or imagine situations of being negatively perceived and disliked by others. This will stifle and limit our possibilities and contacts in life. We react to imaginary situations as if they were real. We will be handicapped in our ability to explore new situations and relationships. We will avoid taking reasonable risks. We will be held in bondage to an irrational fear of an imaginary outside world.

11. Exaggerated sensitivity bears little relationship to reality and therefore it is false. True sensitivity is based on reality, and is one of the strongest forces that promote individual growth and development. It is a most desirable and beautiful human quality. False sensitivity however, often goes together with self-centeredness and an exaggerated sense of self-importance. This is coupled with a relative lack of sensitivity to others and a certain imperviousness to the environment. It leads to thoughtlesness. Exaggerated sensitivity is thus a disguised form of

84

insensitivity. It stifles creativity. True sensitivity promotes creativity. It is often accompanied by a loss of self-consciousness. The self loses its sense of being separate from its surroundings, and is therefore free to explore and create.

12. A basic, unresolved conflict may express itself in all areas of our life. Specifically, it may affect the following:

We may not be able to experience full satisfaction or happiness in anything that we are doing. Actual, concrete achievement will be minimized by the unfulfilled sense of inner calling. Any actual, concrete endeavor or project will seem insignificant or pedestrian relative to our sense of mission. This will inhibit us from fully committing our energies to any concrete task.

Our thinking patterns tend to rigidify. We develop habits of thinking in terms of absolutes, in an either-or, black and white fashion. Options that do not fit preconceived notions are readily dismissed. Our thinking becomes restricted, and less lucid. We will also experience difficulty in developing and forming close human relationships. Our behavior will reinforce our false sensitivity and dependency needs. We find ourselves in a vicious circle from which we are unable to escape. We settle for less than life offers.

3. Habit Formation and Past Conditioning

Repetition and regularity are the basis for habit formation. The essence of habit is the automatic nature of the activity, as for example, personal hygiene or daily routine. We form most of our habits early in life. Habits can be life-enhancing or life- retarding. It is essential that we inculcate constructive habits in our children.

Habit formation becomes more difficult with age. The older we get, the more difficult it is to change negative habits into positive ones, or to acquire new life-asserting habits. Changing old habits requires self-discipline which itself is a function of past habit formation.

We are to a large measure ruled by habits. Constructive habits allow us to put our energies to their most effective use. Destructive habits do just the opposite. They stifle and waste our energies. When we develop constructive habits of thought and behavior we are more free to develop our inner resources, and use them more effectively. We make our habits work for us.

The formation of habits is related to past conditioning, but they are not the same. Habits relate to specific aspects of behavior while past conditioning refers to all our past experiences. The latter is a much broader concept. The quality of our thinking, learning, reading, and comprehending, as well as, the search for truth in ourselves and in others, are all determined by past conditioning.

In the process of growing up we assimilate from the environment certain ways of doing things. We may become sloppy in appearance, posture, and expression, or we may become self-disciplined, and strong. We are often pulled in different directions, but some small event may tip the scale and lead us on a certain course. Once the scale is tipped, the process of reinforcement sets in and we are off into either a growth promoting or growth inhibiting path.

Let us take for example, the quality of learning. The person may have a quick grasp of things, and the ability to learn quickly. The individual however, may fail to develop the habit of thinking through what he or she has learned. The failure to internalize learning causes short retention of the newly acquired material and makes the learning shallow. This is characteristically the case in our schools. We might ask, why is it that so many people with basic intelligence do not develop the habit of thinking through what they have learned, and do not integrate their learning with life experiences? We do not have a simple answer to this question. Our educational system cannot escape however, its share of the blame. Our schools do not foster independent thinking habits, and integrative learning. The average student fails to integrate learning and does not acquire the essential attribute of an educated person. The better students or the more gifted ones may try to correct this deficiency on their own. But they are a relatively small minority.[2]

The conditioning process is continuous in time. As we follow acquired habits or behavior patterns, we reinforce these patterns into our future. The present serves as the link in this interplay between the past and the future. When the past is relatively short, and the future is all before us, when we are young, past conditioning is relatively mild and it is easy to break out from it. Change is comparatively easy. As the past lengthens and the future shortens correspondingly, as we grow older, the past weighs more heavily on us, and change becomes more difficult. To the extent that we are determined by our past, we lose the ability to make free choices. We are prisoners of our past. True freedom however, is primarily to be free from ourselves, that is, from our past fixations and compulsions. (The problem is, how to break undesirable patterns of behavior into desirable ones.) That is where self-discipline and a constructive attitude to life becomes important. Through self-discipline, and the determination to be in control of ourselves, we can change bad habits into good ones, and we can become free from the oppressive weight of our past conditioning.

The ability to lift the weight of our past conditioning has a direct bearing on the question of staying young or of not getting old. Regardless of our chronological age, the question of whether we are relatively young or old depends primarily on the degree to which our future is determined by our past. To the extent that we are not weighted down by our past, but are focused on the future, (and on our freely chosen projects), we retain our youthfulness. This spills over into our physical well- being and appearance. We live longer and look younger. The older we get the more visible is the synchronization between the state of our mind and the state of our body. This is why artificial means to preserve a youthful appearance (cosmetics) often fail. A person who feels old tries to look young. The person becomes less free, and his or her physical well being may be adversely affected.

Life itself does not begin with a free choice. A newborn baby has no past and no conditioning. But the mother's past will intrude itself on the infant and shape his future. Thus life begins with imposed choices. The choices of the newborn baby are not its own. They are those of its mother. As self-consciousness develops, independent choice becomes more possible.

The struggle to be free is an ongoing process of birth and rebirth, where each rebirth occurs on a higher plane, either opening up or foreclosing future choices. To be free is to be able to make choices that enable us to live a fuller life. Free choices reflect our intelligence, values, and experiences without predetermination or compulsion. The sheer weight of the past tends to foreclose certain future possibilities, while experience, wisdom, and intelligence widen the scope of potential choice. To the extent that we conquer the weight of our past and do not allow it to rule our future, to that extent we grow younger in spirit rather than older. Our past turns into a source of light that illuminates our future path. Through the accumulated fund of wisdom, intelligence, and experience, we rise above the petty concerns and fears that loom so large when we are young. Age can become a liberating force in our life, if we are determined to liberate ourselves from the chains of our past fixations and compulsions.

4. The Resolution of Inner Conflict: A Hypothetical Case Study

A basic conflict that is left unresolved for a long time becomes chronic. We learn to live with it, but we are not aware of its real nature. We have not exposed the conflict and brought it to our conscioussness. We may subconsciously adjust or shift the content of the conflict from one area to another. While this gives us us some flexibility, and allows the conflict to adjust its expression to a change in objective reality, the basic conflict remains unresolved. Suppose that the basic conflict is one between the real self and the idealized self.[3] Suppose that the person's idealized self was subconsciously expressed by the person's belief in having a special gift for music. At some point in the person's musical career, he or she may realize that they stand no chance of becoming a great composer or performer. The person may then shift his or her idealized self into another art form, say, dancing. Dancing would now assume all those qualities of the person's idealized self that were formerly associated with music. The basic conflict has changed its expression but retained its nature. A transformation of this kind takes place slowly and gradually as the person comes face to face with reality. It is not a sudden leap. This exemplifies the tenacity with which the person tries to hold on to its idealized self despite the contrary indications in the reality of its situation. There may be several such transformations of the basic conflict throughout the person's life. At the point of each transformation the conflict becomes more acute, but the person manages to conceal it and revert back the conflict into its chronic stage.

At some point however, the person may be ready to confront the problem. This may be the case when the internal conflict has become too burdensome, and the psychosomatic effects noticeable. This ordinarily happens at some critical stage in the person's life, (the so called mid-life crisis.) Certain important events, such as, divorce, remarriage, change of job, profession, or business venture will precipitate the crisis and affect its timing. The person may begin to experience some disturbing symptoms, such as, a sudden disruption in sleep patterns, difficulty in maintaining a given work routine, a lack of enthusiasm in work, and a general decline in vital energy level. The loss of enthusiasm together with a state of intermittent depression will make the person feel chronically tired. The person gradually loses faith in his or her ability to carry out any significant work. Life becomes centered around the physical aspects of living with normal comforts, but the person's sense of future is vanishing. Since the person's idealized self is always future oriented, the diminished sense of the person's future will necessarily expose his or her idealized and illusory self. A loss of faith in the person's future will be experienced as a loss of the essence of life. The person is facing the necessity to restore or reorient his or her basic nature toward accepting the ordinary fate of being human, with all the imperfections and without illusions. Otherwise it becomes difficult to go on with one's life. The individual may now be ready to confront and resolve his or her basic conflict.

Suppose our basic conflict is rooted in our inability to accept a concrete but limited achievement. We have been accustomed to think in global terms. We are unable to make a serious commitment to any concrete project. The time has come whereby we are ready to understand and express the nature of our conflict. Our conflict consists in our semi-conscious desire for a "great" contribution and the impossibility of its realization beforehand. This inner contradiction stifled our freedom to work and to be creative. The conscious recognition of this basic conflict becomes the key to the understanding of secondary or derivative conflicts. The lack of resolution of our basic conflict made it impossible for us to give ourselves fully to anything we were doing. Somehow in our subconscious mind, we were holding back and reserving our full commitment to that globally significant work which we are to undertake in the future. That future work remained however always unspecified, and vague. We could not specify it because subconsciously we realized its lack of realism. The "great endeavor" had to be left vague and allowed to retain a dreamlike quality. The romantic nature of our anticipated future work served as a source of nourishment, sustenance, and comfort to ease the limitations and shortcomings of the present. We could suffer the present through the promise of the future. We created for ourselves a way of living in bad faith. The faith was related to our internalized illusions. We made our own person the object of bad faith. The faith was illusory since it was based on an exaggerated sense of power and self-importance.

Now, in the context of a crisis in our life, this faith has undergone a transformation. It has weakened. The hope and faith in ourselves have diminished. Objective reality has forced itself on us and made us discard our illusions. It made us re-examine our past and acknowledge the unreality of the idealized self. To accept reality is difficult, and we may try to hold on to our illusions for a while longer. This was the underlying cause of the psychosomatic symptoms that we have been experiencing. Ultimately, we are forced to resolve this conflict by accepting objective reality. By accepting ourselves and the reality of our being, we are free to devote our energies to concrete and realizable projects. As we become more engaged in life and free of our basic conflict, the outward manifestations of the conflict together with their corresponding symptoms will also tend to disappear. Pleasures of freedom replace the pains of bondage.

5. Values and Interest

Values do not necessarily express themselves in a person's inclination or interest. Similarly, interest cannot go against our values. If, in our work, we are primarily motivated by extrinsic rewards, we will not be able to fully immerse ourselves in it. The same holds for our values. We will not be able to sustain an intrinsic inclination to an activity or project, if it is contrary to our values. We must believe in what we are doing if we are to enjoy our work. This means that our activity should not conflict with our values. If there is a conflict, our capacities for work will be circumscribed and stunted. We will not be able to enjoy and get excited by what we do.

What can we do in the case where the interest or the activity (work) is in conflict with our values? The resolution of this conflict depends on the nature of our values that conflict with our activity. If these values are important to us to the extent that we would lose self-respect if we compromise them, then we would have to forego the activity or the work rather than compromise our values. If however, these values are not intrinsic to our nature, if they are purely conventional values which we have taken over from the outside without them becoming part of us, (for example, conformity, or the desire for riches, fame, or power), then the conflict will help us revise our values and discard those that are not intrinsic to our nature. Values that are not intrinsic to our nature are false values. False values hold us back in our ability to give ourselves fully to the pursuit of our intrinsic interests.

The choices however, are not clear cut. The knowledge of the relative nature of our values (intrinsic-extrinsic, true-false), and the relative nature of our inclinations (interest-activity) is limited, qualified and uncertain. In the case of existential doubt and uncertainty about everything, our values and our work, it is the determination and the desire to find a way out of the impasse and be true to ourselves, that will lead us in our search for truth. This search entails a readiness to take the risk of not doing the right thing, or of not having the anticipated outcome, as well as, the ability to retain flexibility and change course if we have taken the wrong track. It is equally important not to elevate this flexibility into a virtue per se, and thus be unable to stay with a given course of action long enough to know its true merit. This requres two additional considerations:

1. The need to subject our desires, inclinations or activities to reality testing. Only what is realistically feasible or possible can we include in our desired choice.

2. The need to make decisions and adhere to them.

6. The Making of Decisions

What does it entail for me to have made a decision? It is important that I carry it out. Even if I should get "cold feet" in the midst of carrying out my decision, it is necessary to impose my desire and personal discipline to stay with the decision, however dificult, and not to lose heart.

The only time that I must alter a previous decision is when I have access to significantly new information, or when some basic elements in the situation have changed. That is the meaning of remaining flexible, and retaining a forward adaptability to new developments, new situations, and new opportunities. Discipline, firmness, and adherence to our decisions go hand in hand with openness, vigilance, and alertness to any significant change in the situation, and circumstances that have led to the initial decision. This way we retain flexibility, and can use newly created opportunities to our advantage. We are not held back by self-imposed constraints which do not reflect the given situation any more. A changed situation requires a new adaptation. We need to let go of the old that does not reflect the new. While we have to respect our decisions and adhere to them, we should not be enslaved by them. If we have made a wrong decision, we have to feel free to change it.

7. The Quality of the Decision

We must distinguish between a good decision and a right decision. The first pertains to the quality of the choice, and the other to the nature of the choice. We might not make a superior choice based on a rational evaluation of all available options in terms of their consequences, and the overall costs and benefits involved. If however, our choice is in the direction of our basic goal then the decision is a right decision, regardless of how we have arrived at it. On the other hand, we might have made a superior decision in terms of the process, but if the decision does not fully comply with our basic direction, then it is a wrong decision. A less than optimal decision that is in the right direction is to be preferred to a superior decision that takes us in the wrong direction. The optimality of the decision has to do with the process of how the decision is arrived at. The process is based on a rational evaluation of the available options. Let us briefly enumerate the essential steps connected with rational decision making.

1. On encountering a new situation, we must maintain mental calm. It is important not to give in to anguish, anxiety, or to act compulsively.

2. We must assemble all relevant information that affect the new situation. The information has to be analyzed in terms of its significance, and relative importance. We must be sure that we have sufficiently digested, analyzed and understood the collected information before we make a decision.

3. We need to consider options and courses of action that are available to us. We must anticipate as closely as we can the likely consequences of each available option. It is necessary to estimate as closely as we can the anticipated costs and benefits of each option. The latter includes also the option of postponing or of not making a decision at this time.

4. We must guard against bias in evaluating the relevant information, or of our situation. Personal biases, prejudices, and irrational drives interfere with our ability to see our situation clearly and objectively.

5.   We may be biased in favor of certain outcomes even before we begin the process of decision making. We may exaggerate the importance of those factors that tend to reinforce our bias, and underestimate the importance of what conflicts with our bias. The ability to look at a given situation objectively is of fundamental importance in the art of decision making. We need to be aware of our wishes in order to protect ourselves from them. We must guard against wishful thinking. We cannot let our wishes serve as substitutes for objective and factual information.

6.   In matters of personal choice, we don't normally follow a systematic routine and a rational calculation of costs and benefits. We tend to rely on intuitive judgment. The ability to foresee the consequences of our actions stripped of all wishful thinking means to look at ourselves objectively. Intuition is most effective in guiding our actions when it is based on knowledge, and unbiased information. Only then do we make the best use of our intuitive powers, and let them guide us into the unknown future by what we decide in the present. Every decision entails deciding the unknown future on the basis of incomplete and insufficient information. Intuition is involved in every decision that we make. The greater the impact of a given decision on our life, the greater the importance of a rational and objective approach to the process of making decisions.

7.   The art of personal decision making requires practice. Only through practice can we discover our hidden biases and unexpressed wishes. The wishes that interfere with our vision are nothing but the fear to see clearly what is in front of us. How can we ever get to know what is out there (both within and outside of us) when we are afraid to look? The lure of a fallback into subjective bias is ever present. The practice of unbiased thinking is the only protection agaist bias that we have.

8. Aspirations and the Nature of Our Choices

We have seen that a perfectly arrived at choice in terms of the process can be a bad choice, and an imperfect decision may be a good one. The nature of our choice is conditioned on our knowing what we want, that is, on self-knowledge. The latter requires that we look into our dreams, aspirations, wishes, and hidden preferences openly, and subject them to reality testing. Only then can we find direction. The clearer our goal, the easier the process of making choices. However, in actual life situations we are often motivated by a number of goals, some of which may be in conflict with one another. The conflicting goals or desires operate in our subconscious, and they interfere with the sharpness of our vision. It is necessary to bring all these conflicting goals into the open. We must articulate them, and express them to ourselves. Only then can we sort them out in terms of their importance to our basic direction, and set up the necessary priorities. Clarity of direction and single mindedness of purpose will prevent us from getting bogged down in side issues or being sidetracked in diversion. We need to be vigilant of our primary purpose and not give in to other considerations that seem momentarily attractive, or are easier to pursue.

When we find that we have made a wrong decision, a decision that is inconsistent with our basic purpose, it is imperative that we change course. We must however make sure that this is indeed the case. There is of course no guarantee that the second decision will be a right one. We will have to repeat the process again, and change direction if necessary. We do this until we feel inside of ourselves that we are moving in the right direction. A right decision will always make us feel good about ourselves.

Finally, we come to the most important aspect of the process of decision making. We need to assume full responsibility for our decisions and our actions. The ability, willingness, and readiness to assume responsibility for ourselves can only be acquired and tested by continuous practice. Only through the continuous exercise of personal responsibility for our actions can we gain independence, self-confidence, and self-respect. We cannot blame others for our failures. We are ready to face new situations or unforseen adversity with calmness, self-control, and without fear. Even if the decisions did not turn out as anticipated, we will have gained strength and stature from the knowledge that we have acted in good faith. When we accept responsibility for our mistakes, we learn from them and grow by them. If we don't accept responsibility for our mistakes we will be inclined to repeat them. We need to practice self-discipline without being ruled by it.

94

II. SOCIAL REALITY: EXTERNAL AND CULTURAL TRAPS

As we cannot separate ourselves from our situation, self-knowledge extends itself to the understanding of the nature of the objective reality of our existence. We are often trapped by the conditions of our existence. These traps relate to fear and economic insecurity, a feeling of isolation and powerlessness, exaggerated concern with social status and acquisitions, boredom and submission to mass media, social prejudice, racism, sexism, ageism, and the escape into a private world. The overcoming of the negative conditioning of our culture involves the awareness of our entrapment by it. Traps inhibit our freeedom to act. The person feels dejected and does not know why. "When the mind contemplates its own weakness, it feels pain thereat" (EIII, 55). Dejection "indicates extreme ignorance of self" (EIV, 55), and "extreme infirmity of spirit" (IV, 56). We must be aware of such traps in order to understand them, deal with them, and free ourselves from them.

Only when we understand the nature of the trap we are in, can we overcome it. As we understand the objective conditions of our existence, we become free to act. This does not mean that we can escape our social condition. We live, function, and operate within a reality that is not structured to please us. However, in order to modify or change the conditions of our existence, we must first know them as they are, without prejudice or deception. The true understanding, knowledge, and recognition of the objective condition of our social existence, will turn dejection into its opposite. As we free ourselves from our mental traps, we feel greater power even if there has been no change in the external conditions of our situation. This gives us greater freedom, more reality, and more joy. In what follows, we will illustrate by way of examples, some of the most prevalent existential and cultural traps.

1. Traps at the Work Place

Traps at the work place may take several forms. We may not like our job, or we may feel unappreciated by our superiors. We may be overtaken by anxiety, insecurity, and irrational fear of not performing adequately in our job. We may have a difficult and aggressive boss who is more concerned with power than with quality of service. Bad administrators often hide their professional incompetence or insecurity by their aggressive natures. As administrators they are particularly hard on those who are relatively weak, sensitive or dependent.   On the other hand, we may have an exaggerated sense of self-importance or the importance of our position. We are conscious of our status.   We lose perspective and objectivity as we surround ourselves with status symbols. Or, we may play the power game. We form cliques and play politics with our job. We form a comfortable niche for our security and survival, not realizing that this may turn into a trap. We try to ingratiate ourselves with our superiors in order to advance in the bureaucracy. All such ways of behaving and functioning on the job may act as traps that prevent us from using our physical and mental powers optimally and fully. Most importantly, they may deny us the enjoyment of our work. When we realize the true nature of these handicaps, we understand that they are products of our imagination. The causes of these traps are imaginary. Because of our ignorance of ourselves and of our situation, we are inhibited in our ability to direct ourselves from within, and to be true to ourselves. We cannot fully enjoy our work or give ourselves to it. When we free ourselves from work related anxieties and irrational fear, we can confront arbitrary rule whenever and wherever it occurs. When we test our moral strength by not submitting to fear, we become stronger and freer. We are free to enjoy our work.

2. Powerlessness and Isolation

Feelings of powerlessness and isolation result from the lack of personal involvement in the broader affairs of the community. We feel powerless and alone when our life revolves around our narrow, and selfish interests. We accept and submit voluntarily to extraneous powers that are never fully grasped or understood. We feel that we are spectators on the social scene and not actors.

The essence of power is the ability to make decisions affecting our life and that of others. The political system with its various subsystems represent the macro power-structure. In this system, power tends to be exercised invisibly, and anonymously. People affected by government policies and actions do not face those that exercise power over them directly. It is therefore difficult to assess the impact of a given political decision on one's life. It takes a considerable amount of political sophistication and understanding to be able to do that. It is easier to discern power relationships in the micro-structure, where power is exercised directly, such as in the family, or place of work.

Another way of looking at power is the recognition that power cannot be disassociated from the people (individuals, group or class) that hold it. This means that power will normally be exercised in the interest of the group, class or individuals that hold such power in society. There is no neutral power by definition. Economic and political power cannot be exercised in a vacuum. In the micro-structure power is largely personal. In the macro-structure it is largely impersonal. The ability to trace the locus of power in a given structure is inversely related to the size of the organization.

Powerlessness and isolation have been rationalized and accepted as the normal predicament in modern society. If the condition of the average man in our society is that of isolation and powerlessness, it means that the multitude of people does not exercise its share in the decisions that affect its collective existence. A logical corrolary of this is that such decisions rest with those few who hold and exercise economic and political power in society. It also stands to reason that those who hold power to affect other people's lives prefer to remain invisible, and anonymous. The greater the concentration of economic and political power in a country, the greater the desire for anonimity. The relatively small percentage of inordinate wealth and power holders in a community or nation prefer that this exercise and excessive concentration of power not be well known, understood or analyzed. The rationalization of the so called "human condition", and the concomitant acceptance of the feeling of isolation is a trap by which the very condition of human isolation tends to be perpetuated. "If two come together and unite their strength, they have jointly more power, and consequently more right over nature than both of them separately, and the more there are that have so joined in alliance, the more right they all collectively possess" (Political Treatise, II, 13). People gain power when they join together in the common effort to assert themselves in the political process, and improve the social conditions of their existence. When people understand themselves and the objective conditions of their existence, they are more powerful.

3. Consumerism, Status, and Acquisitions

An exaggerated concern with material acquisitions as the basis for our social status and self-worth act as a trap and a hindrance to our freedom. We are easily manipulated by outside forces, by advertising, and the media. We tend to lose personal discretion in the choices that we make, and become compulsive in our spending behavior. We are given to needless buying. By developing compulsive patterns of spending money on goods that are marginal to our needs, we neglect and inhibit the satisfaction of vital needs in the emotional and spiritual spheres. Compulsive buying habits exaggerate the importance of some needs as against other needs. They trap us into acting against our real needs. Consumerism is a direct consequence of alienation, and the corresponding estrangement of life from work.

The divorce of work from life is at the root of alienation. The estrangement of people from their work is perhaps the most basic problem of modern society. Since work does not provide people with an outlet for their absorbing and creative powers, the individual loses the connection to his or her vital self. People get to be disconnected, divided, and estranged from themselves. Instead of affirming ourselves in our work, we deny ourselves in it. Productive life, life's most essential activity, and life itself, turn into a means of life. When we are estranged from our life activity, from our essential nature, and from our humanity, we are also estranged from those around us. We come to be ruled by things, not by our natures. Our existence becomes reified.[4] The reification of consciousness can be seen even in education. Education has been reduced to commodity production. The objective is to prepare people to function in the workplace, a workplace that has been emptied of human essence. Teachers and students have become reduced in the educational process to a mere routine functioning.[5] There is little true learning, no real excitement, no joy of learning, and no striving for excellence in our educational system. Our education is symptomatic of the commercialization of our culture.

Many of the cultural values and images propagated by advertising and certain segments of TV entertainment are directly or indirectly designed to dull people's intellect, and make them subject to easy manipulation. Advertising based on the appeal to the unrefined instincts of the multitude, lowers the people's level of sophistication, and inhibits their ability to think freely. People are unable to form independent judgments about their social existence. Much of the advertising and sensationalized mass media breed baseness of character and vulgarity of taste. It fosters prejudice, superstition, and violence. It acts as a very effective block on people's freedom to chart their life according to their inner needs and beliefs. It is very difficult to resist the all pervasive commercialization of culture. The constant exposure to advertising and TV culture weakens people's awareness of their true inner needs and desires. Eventually, people lose the sense of individuality, aliveness, and purpose. Boredom sets in as the normal condition of daily life. Watching television becomes habitual and mechanical. The people are not even aware of their boredom.

4. Social Prejudice

Prejudice is when one generalizes from an individual experience of pain or pleasure caused by a stranger to that of an entire nation or class of people. "If a man has been affected pleasurably or painfully by anyone, of a class or nation different from his own, and if the pleasure or pain has been accompanied by the idea of the said stranger as cause, under the general category of class or nation: the man will feel love or hatred, not only to the individual stranger, but also to the whole class or nation whereto he belongs" (EIII, 56). Social prejudice is usually associated with painful, and discriminatory practices toward minorities and groups of people. Social prejudice is not only pernicious in its effect on other people, but more than anything else, it is most harmful to the individuals themselves. Prejudice hinders free thinking and open-mindedness. The tendency to dogmatic thinking and to a set of rigid values inhibits our ability to see relevant or significant aspects of any problem that we encounter in life. Our vision is limited and our reasoning power is diminished. We do not question or reflect upon anything that does not fit in with our preconceived notions. We become prisoners of our dogmas. Consider how difficult it is, to free ourselves from ingrained sexist attitudes, and how they inhibit our ability to love and experience happiness with another person.

Similarly, with other group prejudices. Racial prejudice and prejudice against older people is more widespread in our society than anyone is willing to admit. The destructive impact of prejudicial thinking and behavior falls ultimately on the prejudiced individuals themselves. Let us look at a child who is free of prejudice. The child is free and natural in his encounter with other people. He does not differentiate between black people and white people, old people or young people. He is not yet burdened by the need to accept or reject anybody because of social prejudice or culturally absorbed stereotypes. The child is free to enjoy and give itself fully to the activity at hand. Few people grow up and retain that remarkable quality of innocence to accept others for what they are (for their character) and not for who they are. When people grow up, their behavior becomes cramped, forced, and unfree. Prejudiced and stereotyped behavior creeps into every act of people's most casual dealings with others. Thus, grown up people tend to lose aliveness and spontaneity.

Inhibiting influences that emanate from an alienated culture and from economic insecurity make people retreat into loneliness and isolation. To compensate for the feeling of helplessness and powerlessness, individuals withdraw into a world of make-believe and pretense. People tend to lose the sense of self-worth based on inner aliveness and productiveness. They supplant it with the need to act superior, being "smart", making jokes at the expense of others, and by the conspicuous accumulation of gadgets. Self-worth built on having rather than on being is bound to be short-lived and shallow. No matter how many gadgets one accumulates, there is always going to be someone who has more. The same holds for all externalities (fame, honor, power, or riches). "There is no individual thing in nature, than which there is not another more powerful and strong. Whatsoever thing be given, there is something stronger whereby it can be destroyed" (EIV, Axiom). There is no end to the competitve race. In the end, it wears people out. By the time people realize the futility of living for the sake of things rather than for the sake of themselves, it is often too late. The futility of the competitive race dawns on them, and along with it the realization that not even in material things do they have a lot to show for. A life spent in the competitive race brings little security to the person. It leads to disillusionment, and to a sense of being cheated. Frustration and nagging doubts about the person's integrity and self-worth set in. This happens often when the person is caught up in the mid-life crisis. The average middle-class, middle-age person realizes his or her fragile existence. But a crisis is also an opportunity and a challenge. The individual may lose interest in life, or may find renewed meaning in life. People may retreat from life into the private world of mass entertainement and alcohol addiction, or they may confront themselves and get to know themselves. "Reason demands that every man should love himself and should seek what is useful to him" (EIV, 18, Schol.). "Dejection is a sign of extreme self-ignorance and of extreme infirmity of spirit" (EIV, 55 and 56). "Yet dejection can be more easily corrected than pride; for the latter being a pleasurable emotion, and the former a painful emotion, the pleasurable is stronger than the painful" (EIV, 56, Note). A crisis in life is an opportunity for self-examination and self-renewal, whereby life-asserting forces prove stronger and overcome the life-denying forces. "Desire arising from pleasure is, other conditions being equal, stronger than desire arising from pain" (EIV, 18).

III. THE INDIVIDUAL AND THE STATE

1. The State Exists for the People

Spinoza's fundamental political premise is that the state exists for the people, and is to serve the needs of the people. The state should not be considered an entity separate and apart from the people. No action or policy of the state can be justified on the basis of "reason of State" as distinct from the interests and the needs of the people that make up the state. The function of the state is to guarantee people's rights to live in peace and security, and to provide the necessary conditions for the full development of all. The state is to protect the civic liberties and the rights of all the citizens. The aim is to equalize opportunity for all the people, and to insure that people's actions are guided by enlightened self interest rather than by envy, greed, and passion. Enlightened self interest dictates that people help each other, cooperate with each other, trust one another, and treat each other with fairness and justice. This insures peace, harmony, and cooperation between people. When people act on the basis of long term interest rather than short term advantage, they feel secure in their dealings with each other. "We may, under the guidance of reason, seek a greater good in the future in preference to a lesser good in the present, and we may seek a lesser evil in the present in preference to a greater evil in the future "(EIV, 66). However, human beings are more prone to be driven by envy, greed, and passion rather than by reason and enlightened self interest. "Yet it rarely happens that men live in obedience to reason...."(EIV,35 Note). This is why laws are necessary. The laws of the state are designed to enable people to live together in harmony, cooperate with each other, and to make them "refrain from all actions which can injure their fellow-men" (EIV, 37, Note). "Such a society established with laws and the power of preserving itself is called a *State*, while those who live under its protection are called *citizens* " (Ibid.).

Democracy is the most natural form of government since it serves best the interests of the people. The aim of a democratic state is to insure the freedom, and the well being of all its citizens. People's fundamental rights to live in security, peace, and harmony are best protected in a democracy. Freedom of speech and the tolerance of opposing views are basic to the functioning of a democratic state. The tolerance of political opposition, diversity of opinion, and the guarantee of freedom of speech, is a necessary pre-condition for peaceful resolution of conflict. This assures rationality and stability of the state. A democratic state expresses the will of the people, guarantees the security and the liberty of its citizens, and makes the people the masters of their collective well being. Democracy is also the best protection against war, because war does not serve the interest of the people. Individual rulers or military men may gain honors or riches from war, but the people suffer and become empoverished by war.

Political liberties in democracy are derived from the freedom of the people. Freedom can never be based on fear. "He who is led by fear, and does good in order to escape evil, is not led by reason" (EIV,63). The purpose of democratic government is to bring about a free society based on reason, not on fear. "The man who is guided by reason is more free in a state, where he lives under a general system of law, than in solitude, where he is independent" (EIV, 73).

Freedom of opinion is fundamental to the stability of the state. Spinoza is against all forms of totalitarian rule; "a man's loyalty to the state should be judged, like his loyalty to God, from his actions only - namely from his charity towards his neighbours;...free thought is itself a virtue... it cannot be crushed... it is absolutely necessary for progress in science and the liberal arts..."[6] A totalitarian state is unstable because, "laws directed against opinions affect the generous-minded rather than the wicked....they cannot be maintained without great peril to the state....Moreover, such laws are almost always useless, for those who hold that the opinions proscribed are sound, cannot possibly obey the law.... He that knows himself to be upright....shrinks from no punishment..."[7] "In democracy, (the most natural form of government) everyone submits to the control of authority over his actions, but not over his judgment and reason; that is, seeing that all cannot think alike, the voice of the majority has the force of law, subject to repeal if circumstances bring about a change of opinion. In proportion as the power of free judgment is withheld we depart from the natural condition of mankind, and consequently the government becomes more tyrannical."[8] Therefore people must guard their freedoms and be vigilant against any usurpation of it by the authorities.

True happiness is non-exclusive; "to man there is nothing more useful than man...men who are governed by reason,...desire for themselves nothing, which they do not also desire for the rest of mankind, and, consequently, are just, faithful, and honourable in their conduct" (EIV,18, Note). The state would be superfluous if people would follow reason. The multitude however is driven by passion not reason. Its impulses and urges are based on *imaginatio*, not on *ratio*. It is therefore unstable, shifty, and subject to vacillation between conflicting emotions. This leads to fanaticism, intolerance, superstition, cruelty, and violence. "The crowd plays the tyrant, when it is not in fear;"(EIV,54, Note). The authority and power of the state is necessary to make people's actions comply with the precepts of reason. Fear of punishment and obedience to authority will insure right conduct. Religion should be used to make the multitude pious, devout, fearful, and law abiding. While emotions of hope and fear are not by themselves good (EIV,47), people will thus behave as if they were following the guidance of reason. "As men seldom live under the guidance of reason, these two emotions, namely Humility and Repentance, as also Hope and Fear, bring more good than harm; hence, as we must sin, we had better sin in that direction...." (EIV, 54, Note).

2. The Question of Justice

Reason and justice have been subjected to intellectual derision and cynical abuse by all sorts of people, usually by the protagonists of the Status Quo and rationalizers of existing injustice. For "those that cry out the loudest against the misuse of honour and the vanity of the world, are those who most greedily covet it"(EV,10, Note). Spinoza expresses faith in the power of reason to prevail over unreason. "Let satirists then laugh their fill at human affairs, let theologians rail, and let misanthropes praise to their utmost the life of untutored rusticity, let them heap contempt on men and praises on beasts; when all is said, they will find that men can provide for their wants much more easily by mutual help, and that only by uniting their forces can they escape from the dangers that on every side beset them:...." (EIV, 35, Note).

Justice and injustice are not categories of nature. Nature always follows its own laws. Concepts of justice or injustice are to be applied only to human institutions and social arrangements. Good or evil, justice or injustice cannot be attributed to the state of nature. Suppose a child is born blind. As an act of nature, the child's blindness is neither just nor unjust. "We may readily understand that there is in the state of nature nothing, which by universal consent is pronounced good or bad;....In the state of nature, therefore, sin is inconceivable; it can only exist in a state, where good and evil are pronounced on by common consent,....there is nothing in the state of nature answering to justice and injustice. Such ideas are only possible in a social state, when it is decreed by common consent what belongs to one and what to another"(EIV, 37, Note II).

Only what can be changed by society or by the institutions devised by human beings can be deemed just or unjust. Suppose that the child's vision could have been restored through early medical attention. If the necessary medical treatment was denied to the child for reasons of poverty, ignorance or lack of funds to pay for the hospital (lack of medical insurance), then an injustice was done to the child. For,"providing for the poor is a duty, whch falls on the State as a whole, and has regard only to general advantage"(EIV, App. 17). The neglect or unavailability of the necessary medical intervention led to a life long condemnation of the child to blindness. Society had the means to prevent it, but social organization through its existing institutions denied justice to the newborn baby. Let us take another example: Suppose a child is denied the proper nutrition necessary for its development. Physical and emotional care for the child is a parental responsibility. But what if the parents are poor and out of work, and therefore cannot provide the needed food for their child? Does the child still have a claim to basic nutrition for a healthy development? The child is not the cause of the parents' unemployment and lack of income. Moreover, assume that there are enough resources in society to provide for the basic needs for all its members. Then poverty and unemployment are matters of defective social organization and resource distribution. In this case, injustice was done first to the child, (the child did not do anything to cause the denial of its basic nutritional needs), and secondarily, justice was denied to the parents by their inability to find employment. Injustice in this case has been compounded to child and parents. Parents and child have been punished for no particular wrong doing. The inability to find employment is a form of punishment.[9] The same can be extended into any practice of economic and social discrimination. The system's failure to enforce its non-discriminatory laws is also a contravention of justice. (In general, we may say that an act of injustice occurs when consequences are not the results of the sufferer's deeds.)

In a truly democratic state, reason is identified with justice. The enlightened self-interest of a collectivity of people, a nation or community of nations, coincides with justice for all its members. "The good which every man, who follows after virtue, desires for himself he will also desire for other men, and so much the more, in proportion as he has a greater knowledge of God" (EIV, 37). And, "The free man never acts fraudulently, but always in good faith" (EIV, 72). The identification of collective reason with social justice rests on the proposition that the collective welfare of all is enhanced by the optimum contribution of each to the common good. The common good or the public interest embraces all people within the collectivity. (Individual good refers to the private interests of the people within the group.) However, within any given community of people, the distribution of power and material resources is uneven. Social reality consists in dominance of some people over others. If there is an unequal sharing of power, and if certain groups of people are effectively excluded from access to power in society, the notion of the "common good" remains an abstract notion. Therefore the concept of the "common good" presupposes real democracy within the social order. In such democracy, power is not the exclusive privilege and possession of some members as against others. In a truly democratic society, the welfare of all is enhanced by the welfare of each. All people have access to opportunity for personal well-being, individual growth, and development. The right to life, liberty, and happiness is guaranteed by the collective will of the people. The dignity of the human being is its highest expression. Any diminution of the person or any indignity inflicted on any one individual is a matter of highest concern for the people, since all people are diminished by it. Therefore, it cannot be tolerated.

A society where real democracy prevails is a society governed by reason. "In so far only as men live in obedience to reason, do they always necessarily agree in nature" (EIV, 35). "There is no individual thing in nature, which is more useful to man, than a man who lives in obedience to reason" (Ibid. Schol.). In such a society, the interests of all people and the interests of each person coincide. In an ideal democracy, the "common good" is consistent with the individual good. Each person benefits from the contribution of others. The common good is served best by facilitating the optimum development of all the people. A democratic social order is to ensure the freedom and the optimum development of all the people. The function of the state is to make the multitude follow reason. The state is to guarantee equal access to opportunity, and create the conditions for a full life for all its citizens. People everywhere have the same common interests: To provide for their basic needs and to establish the necessary material conditions to enable each person to be free to develop their innate potentialities; To enhance people's creative powers, and provide an opportunity for each to make a productive contribution to the common good; To enable human beings to lead a rich, and meaningful life; To let people enjoy the fruits of their labor, and know the real joys of life in their magnanimity and infinity; And most of all, to allow each person to live in peace and security. While this is an idealized view of a democratic society, it nevertheless shows the direction to which collective reason points to.

Notes

1. See, Herbert Benson, *Beyond the Relaxation Response*, New York: The Berkley Publishing Group, 1985. See also, Thich Nhat Hanh, *The Miracle of Mindfulness: A Manual on Meditation*, Boston: Beacon Press, 1987.
2. Lewis Schipper, "Innovative Teaching," in *Improving College and University Teaching*, Vol.32, Winter 1984.
3. Karen Horney, *Neurosis and Human Growth*, New York: Norton, 1950.
4. Georg Lukacs, *History and Class Consciousness*. Cambridge, Massachusetts: The MIT Press, 1971.
5. Ohmer Milton, *Alternatives to the Traditional: How Professors Teach and Students Learn*. San Francisco: Josey Bass, 1972. pp.128-129.
6. A Theologico-Political Treatise, Chap. XX. *The Chief Works of Benedict De Spinoza*, transl. by R.H.M. Elwes, vol. I. p.261.
7. Ibid., pp.262-263.
8. Ibid., pp.263-264.
9. Lewis Schipper, *A Guaranteed Employment System in the United States*, Washington, D. C.: Howard University Research Monograph, 1967.

CHAPTER 7
THE WAY TO SELF- KNOWLEDGE

1. Telos in Nature And in Human Beings

The question of final causes in nature takes us back to Aristotle. For Aristotle, to know a thing is to understand its causes (material, formal, efficient, and final causes). He defines the final cause as "the end, that for the sake of which a thing is; health is the cause of walking" (Metaphysics Book V, 1013 a 34-35).

The phrase "the end ... for the sake of which" has been misinterpreted by the Schoolmen of the Middle Ages, as that for which the thing was created by the divine Creator and given a purpose or end to it. The end in nature was to serve man, as its highest expression. Thus, God created nature for the sake of man, and the purpose of man is to worship God. This interpretation of Aristotle by the Schoolmen Spinoza ridicules: "There is no need to show at length, that nature has no particular goal in view, and that final causes are mere human figments" (EI, App.). The Schoolmen identified final causes with efficient causes and used them as arguments for the existence of a Creator, (the argument from design). For Aristotle, natural ends are immanent in nature. The *telos* of the thing is to actualize its nature. Natural ends are powers *(dynameis)* inherent in each thing striving to actualize themselves in activity *(energeia)*. The nature of man is to be healthy (in body and mind), and one of the ways to actualize this "telos" is through exercise (walking, etc.).

This is much the same as Spinoza's *conatus*, or the endeavor of the thing to persevere in its nature. The *telos* (striving, *conatus*) of a thing is to be all that its nature (essence) allows it to be. The *telos* of a thing is the actualization of its potential. The "telos" of an acorn is to grow into a mighty oak tree, just as my "telos" is to realize the full potential imbued in my innate essence. For Spinoza, the essence of man is both innate as well as formed (conceived) in actual existence. "For, by a modification of man's essence, we understand every disposition of the said essence, whether such disposition be innate, or whether it be conceived solely under the attribute of thought, or solely under the attribute of extension, or whether lastly, it be referred simultaneously to both these attributes"(EIII, Def. I, Expl.).

The most fundamental meaning of freedom is the freedom to be. It means the actualization of the inherent powers within us in order to become all that we can be. Whatever interferes with this actualization is a limitation on our freedom. These limitations are internal (our passions), and external (limits imposed on our free development by the environment). The environment may be conducive in different degrees, that is, it can be more or less helpful, to our optimal development. If the child does not get its proper physical and emotional nurture, it will be stunted in its normal growth. It is like the acorn not getting enough nourishment to develop into a tree.

If we consider the complexity and multiplicity of needs whose satisfaction are necessary for the optimum development of mind and body, and how, throughout the process of growth, we may be deprived of these needs, (whether it be at home, in school, in the street or through the culture and an oppressing environment), we come to realize , that all of us grow up, in unfreedom rather than in freedom. By the time we are grown, we may already not be free to make the kind of choices that will further our well being and enhance our freedom "to be all we can be." We may already be so fully determined that we are unable and unwilling to understand the internal impediments (the causes of our passions), and the external constraints (environmental limitations) upon our freedom. This is unfortunately the lot of the multitude of the people. Freedom for the multitude is by and large the freedom to make meaningless choices.

Since life itself will always impose limits to our freedom, we can never be absolutely free, or unfree. We can only be more free or less free. In the process of living we can either enlarge or curtail the realm of our freedom. To the extent that we are determined from the outside, we become less free. To the extent that we actively determine ourselves, we become more free. Every free act makes another free act more likely. Conversely, every unfree act makes another unfree act more likely. Thus, freedom and unfreedom tend to be cumulative in their effects. The more each is allowed to endure, the more difficult it is to change direction. It is as difficult for the free person to become unfree as it is difficult for the unfree person to become free. Since people for the most part live in unfreedom, and since unfreedom is a painful emotion, they are inclined to disguise their unfreedom and rationalize it into a form of freedom, namely, the freedom to make hollow choices.

It follows that the road to freedom leads through the awareness of our internal and external impediments to it. The awareness of our unfreedom is a necessary condition for becoming more free (for the exercise of our freedom). This necessary awareness extends itself to all areas of our existence, (the physical, material, intellectual, spiritual, emotional, aesthetic, and moral spheres of life). Thus, the striving to be, if it is not to be a blind striving, but one that leads to an enlargement of our freedom lies in our understanding of ourselves, of our environment and of the society in which we live. Only through understanding can we begin to realize our "freedom to be all we can be". This understanding is nothing but the activation of the mind in forming clear and distinct ideas of what was formerly perceived passively and confusedly, through the imagination. We begin with the understanding of our needs.

2. Human Needs and Their Satisfaction

Spinoza is explicit on the basic needs of human beings. This is expressed in the following quotation, which I quote at length, since this matter is often misinterpreted or misunderstood by his commentators:

"Those things are most useful which can so feed and nourish the body, that all its parts may rightly fulfill their functions. For in proportion as the body is capable of being affected in a great number of ways, so much the more is the mind capable of thinking. But there seem to be very few things of this kind in nature; wherefore for the due nourishment of the body we must use many foods of diverse nature. For the human body is composed of very many parts of different nature which stand in continual need of varied nourishment, so that the whole body may be equally capable of doing everything that can follow from its own nature, and consequently that the mind also may be equally capable of forming many perceptions" (EIV, App. 27).

"it is the part of a wise man to refresh and to recreate himself with moderate and pleasant food and drink, and also with perfumes, with the soft beauty of growing plants, with dress, with music, with many sports, with theaters, and the like, such as every man may make use of without injury to his neighbour " (EIV, 45, Note).

"they who know the true use of money, and who fix the measure of wealth solely with regard to their actual needs, live content with little " (EIV, App. 29).

The passages show that for us to live and function optimally in body and mind, we must be able to satisfy our basic needs for food, clothing, housing, health, education, work, etc.[1] Such needs are culturally and historically determined. What once may have been a luxury, becomes a basic need in a different stage of the development of mankind. Body and mind develop in the process of interaction, activity and work, "no one has hitherto laid down the limits to the powers of the body" (EIII, 2, Note.), or to the mind.

The process of human history is the process of creation and satisfaction of human needs through labor. Hegel and Marx both developed this point further. Its origin is to be found in Spinoza. Hegel saw human labor and human activity in general, as projections of man's consciousness. For Hegel, the concrete historical process plays itself out primarily on the plane of consciousness. For Marx, labor is also the essence of the historical process, but it takes place in the concrete world, by creating objects that satisfy people's needs. Human beings exercise their drives and their natural powers in their interaction with nature. Through labor, we develop our powers (forces of production) as well as our needs. Our needs and the means for their satisfaction are historically conditioned. Human needs pertain to all the areas of our life (consumption, production, work, and social interactions). They condition and are conditioned by each other.

In each area of need are threshold points below which the optimum functioning of body and mind becomes impaired or negatively affected. Such thresholds are themselves culturally and historically determined. On the physical and material plane, the lack of need satisfaction is directly felt by anyone living below the assumed poverty line. Such first order needs, or what Maslow calles deficiency needs,[2] are directly experienced in consciousness. Their satisfaction takes priority and is a precondition for the satisfaction of our higher order needs. The function of the State is to assure a minimum level of material need satisfaction for the poor. For "to give aid to every poor man, is far beyond the power and the advantage of any private person....Hence providing for the poor is a duty which falls on the State as a whole, and has regard only to the general advantage" (EIV, App.17).

The freedom of individuals to fully develop their faculties (to be all they can be) requires that their basic needs are met. This idea becomes instrumental in defining a basic need. An essential need is one that if not met, the person will be stunted in the development towards a free human being. Needs vary with age, the strength of their effect, and the likely reversibility of the adverse impact of need deprivation at a later time. The most serious consequences of need deficiencies occur before the person reaches maturity. At a young age, basic needs must be met by the family. At adulthood, they must be met by the individuals themselves. Such needs include caring and providing for their families. Whether and to what extent individuals are able to provide the basic needs of their own and those of their families depends on the degree of their awareness of such needs. Need awareness is a fundamental aspect of self- knowledge and a precondition for human freedom. The way to freedom lies in the understanding of our condition and the causes behind it.

Let us take the household as a case in point. The household is the most basic social unit. It is an organized arrangement with a division of functions between its parts in order to fulfill certain basic material and emotional needs for its members. Optimally, it should provide a suitable environment for the rearing of children, love and emotional security for the family members, and an outlet for venting the frustrations of daily life. To the extent that the household meets these needs, it enhances the potential well being of all its members. We may call it a well functioning household.

Since a variety of needs have to be met by the household, a given household may function well in one sense and poorly in another. A household may provide for the material needs and perhaps in excess of such needs for all its members, yet at the same time be utterly deficient in giving warmth, affection, and emotional security to the family. The overall effect of such a household, characterized by material affluence and emotional neglect may well be detrimental to all of its members. We are all familiar with high pressure executives who are so consumed with their work and with money making that they have little time left for anything else, including their families. Spinoza expresses this:

"But money has furnished us with a token of everything; hence it is with this notion of money that the mind of the multitude is chiefly engrossed" (EIV, App.28). Most people are concerned with money and they associate pleasure with money, "nay, it can hardly conceive any kind of pleasure, which is not accompanied with the idea of money as a cause" (ibid.).

Spinoza further says that neither the miser nor the spendthrift understands his real needs. The one seeks money for its own sake (to keep and accumulate). He does not spend enough on his bodily needs or the cultivation of his mind. The other identifies all pleasure with money. It is the free man who knows "the true use of money, and who seeks wealth solely with regard to his actual needs." He is thereby content with little.

The causes for obsessive work (so-called workaholics) and the corresponding exaggerated needs for spending or saving, are for the most part external. They are fixations (passions) based on imagination and confused ideas about the nature of real needs. Only wise people understand the nature of their needs and determine them internally, that is from within themselves. Their mind is active and self-determining, which causes their needs never to be exaggerated. Since their needs are not excessive, their wants are few, and they derive real pleasure from their satisfaction. The satisfaction of their true needs enables them to affect and be affected optimally by the environment and by the other people around them. Wise people make full use of their needs to grow and develop in mind and body. They are not given to outside pressures to spend or save by advertising or by conspicuous consumption. They determine themselves the level of prudent spending and are therefore independent, free, and happy.

In Spinoza's reference to the multitude equating everything (need and pleasure) with money, in its substituting quantity of money for quality of need, thus confusing having things with being somebody, we have the germ of what Marx later called "commodity fetishism" under capitalism. Capitalist production is production of exchange value, and the place of the producer in it is not as clear as when products are being produced for their use value, that is for direct consumption. Commodity production is veiled under a cloak of mystery. In it, *social relations between man assume the fantastic form of relations between things."* [3] As in primitive religion where people attach magical qualities to inert objects and make them articles of worship (called idols or fetishes), so do commodities in capitalism become objects of idolatry, due to the enigmatic nature of their production. Through the magic of money, money being commodity's most generalized form, life becomes inverted. Instead of people ruling over things, things rule over people. People's existence becomes reified. Relations between people assume the form of relations between things, and relations between things mask relations between people. If, we hold with Marx, that consciousness is first of all the consciousness of one's existence, and if one's existence is thought of in terms of things, then consciousness itself becomes reified under the capitalist mode of production. This confusion of having with being, or the need to consume and buy in order to impress others (conspicuous consumption) with inner happiness and freedom (true being), has become embedded in capitalist culture. Commodity fetishism is behind the pervasive phenomenon of alienation in modern society.

The incipient tendency of the multitude to superficial ways of living and its lack of understanding of the beauty of life and the complexity of human needs (not all of them involving money), was raised to one of the pillars of capitalist production. Under capitalism, new objects constantly turn into new needs, thus enabling capitalist production to expand.[4] There is an inversion of quality (true need) into quantity (exaggerated and false needs). "The quantity of money becomes its sole effective quality."[5] Compare Marx's statement above with Spinoza, EIV, App. 28, "the multitude can hardly conceive any kind of pleasure, which is not accompanied with the idea of money as a cause." The early stage of commercial capitalism was already well established in seventeenth century Holland.

Marx's subsequent vision of a communist society, where people will be free to develop and pursue their sensual, intellectual, emotional, and aesthetic capabilities to the enrichment of all; where people's higher order needs (needs to develop the creative potential in all areas of human endeavor) will check any excessive material wants; and where production in the form of associated producers will provide for people's necessary material needs, was greatly influenced by Spinoza's community of free human beings. Spinoza's community of free men inspired Marx's vision of the future communist society, where freedom from want would become fully realized, and the freedom to create and self express would become our true need. In such a society man will be an end in himself and the quality of life will be found in fulfilling human relationships rather than in domination and competition. This utopian vision of Marx can be traced back to Jewish Messianism which is also at the root of Spinoza's community of free human beings. The difference, however, between Marx and Spinoza is this: Spinoza emphasized individuals' responsibility for their own freedom, and he didn't think that freedom can be imposed from above. He was sceptical about the multitude's ability to become free. Marx, on the other hand, made history itself (in its various modes and relations of production) progress toward freedom. Through his extraordinary deep insight into capitalist reality and in his vision of a future communist society, Marx has bequeathed to posterity, a faith not in the outcome of history but in the possibilities of history. That faith together with his powerful tools of social analysis has proven to be a tremendous force in the shaping of history. Its repercussions still reverberate everywhere today, although Marxist states have suddenly collapsed. Marx and Spinoza were both the greatest realists and the greatest believers. History nevertheless confirms Spinoza rather than Marx. It moves toward affirming the possibilities for human beings to lie in the individual rather than in the collective. The greatest fault of socialist societies lies in the neglect of the individual's freedom, in the crippling of individual initiative, and in the non-recognition of people's need for spiritual and moral elevation. They failed to understand that it is the free person that makes the community of free people possible. Given the repercussions and the convulsions that are taking place in many socialist societies today, the verdict of history is inclined more toward the affirmation of Spinoza rather than Marx.

After this digression into history and the historical process, we come back to the individuals and their needs.

3. Body Awareness and Health Needs

In the area of preventive medicine and body awareness, Spinoza was also far ahead of his contemporaries. Only recently have we come to appreciate his full impact on holistic medicine. Spinoza's reference to the optimum level of "motion and rest" in the different bodily parts requires us to be in tune with our bodies. We need to develop a way of listening to our body for its state of health. We should listen to the body's messages and correctly perceive and interpret the warning signals emanating from it.

The emphasis is on the development of good habits and a healthy life style. To be able to prevent a sickness is more basic than to cure it. Holistic medicine is based on the uniqueness of the individual and his or her non-identification with the average. The average, however, is what modern medicine operates on. Everybody is reduced to the average. While this enables quick treatment and mass health care, it is also a source of many health problems that the individual medical practitioner is unable to detect and therefore is likely to misdiagnose. This puts greater responsibility on the individuals themselves to look out for their health needs in order to prevent disease. The awareness of proper health needs will induce the person to cultivate a life style that is conducive to optimum state of bodily and mental health. The person will avoid bodily excesses that stimulate one part of the body at the expense of other parts, or at the expense of the body as a whole. He or she will avoid indulging in excesssive food, sex, or any other forms of compulsive behavior. Similarly, the person will not get carried away with mental exaggerations reflecting the corresponding bodily exaggerations. Such exaggerations lead to suffering and pain. (Stimulation and suffering are attributed to persons when one part of their nature is more affected than the rest.) When all parts are affected alike, the result is merriment or melancholy. And, "mirth cannot be excessive, but is always good; contrarywise, Melancholy is always bad" (EIV, 42).

Progressive inattention to body signals and lack of their awareness may lead to a breakdown in body functioning and disease. The ancient Greeks viewed disease as a disturbance in the balance of the fluids in the body. Similarly, Spinoza regards disease as a change in "motion and rest" in parts of the body relative to the whole. The latter is also an imbalance similar to that recognized by the Greeks. Correspondingly, health is viewed as the maintenance of the proper balance and the harmonious interplay between the different bodily parts (fluids, motion and rest, etc.) and the whole.

The free person will be sensitive to any cues emanating from the body and will know how to listen and interpret early warning signals. He or she will take proper measures (including a change in life style if necessary), to prevent the onset of disease. Bodily awareness itself should not be exaggerated. Exaggerated body awareness will turn the individual into a hypochondriac. That is the other side (and therefore the equivalent) of complete bodily insensitivity. Exaggeration of any kind is equally bad for the well being (freedom) of body and mind. In this Spinoza comes close to the Aristotelian notion of virtue as the mean between the corresponding extremes of character.

If however we are struck by sickness or personal tragedy, the free human being "is scarcely at all disturbed in spirit" (EV, 42,Schol.), and here Spinoza comes closest to the Stoa:

"We shall bear with an equal mind all that happens to us in contravention to the claims of our own advantage, as long as we are conscious, that we have done our duty, and that the power which we possess is not sufficient to enable to protect ourselves completely; remembering that we are part of universal nature, and that we follow her order. If we have a clear and distinct understanding of this, that part of our nature which is defined by intelligence, in other words, the better part of ourselves will assuredly acquiesce in what befalls us, and in such acquiescence will endeavor to persist" (EIV, App. 32).

Spinoza emphasizes a truth that is obvious to the free person but not obvious to the common person, that human needs can only be provided by the cooperation of many people, which means, that people need each other more than anything else. "Now for providing these nourishments, the strength of each individual would hardly suffice, if men did not lend one another mutual aid" (EIV, App. 28).

Spinoza is clear about the limitation of human existence and that the exaggerated preoccupation with one kind of need (money) will crowd out the person's higher level needs, or what Maslow calls, meta-needs. These are our spiritual and cultural needs, our needs for beauty, goodness of heart, wholeness, justice, and order. The satisfaction of our spiritual and cultural needs enable us to achieve peak experiences.[6] Such needs are just as real as the physical needs, and when these are not satisfied, we cannot be happy. Maslow's model of a hierarchy of needs can also be traced back to Spinoza (EIV, 45, Note). There is a hierarchy of needs from the physical to the artistic and to the spiritual plane. Our highest happiness (*beatudo*) comes from the satisfaction of our spiritual needs. For Spinoza, the possibility of people's true happiness is not relegated to some distant future (Marx' s communist state or the Messianic vision of the Old Testament), but it is given to the wise person in the present. Admittedly, this limits the possibility of freedom to the select few rather than to the many. However, Spinoza is not an elitist in the sense that he precludes the possibility of individual advancing from the bondage of the multitude to the freedom of the select. Such a road is open to everyone. Everybody has the ability to understand himself and God.

Spinoza has often been called an elitist, but I find this designation a false one. We must differentiate between two meanings of the concept of "elite". The first meaning is descriptive of a group's (collectivity, nation, society,) actual distribution of its population with respect to any desirable characteristic, whether of character, power, wealth, intelligence, or ability. In this sense, the designation of an "elite" indicates the actual division of the population between the few (exceptionally able, wealthy, powerful, strong,) and the many who don't exhibit this characteristic. The term "elite" as used here is an objective description of an actual state of affairs, or of the reality of a given situation, without any expression of a value judgment or of personal preference. The second meaning of the term "elite" pertains to the personal preference of the individual thus designated. To be an elitist in this sense means to want to perpetuate the given state of affairs and to approve of it. It refers to members of a given privileged group that want to safeguard their privilege and exclude others from any access to it. Unfortunately, people confound the two meanings of the word. To be an elitist in the first sense simply means to be a realist. Spinoza was a realist. However, it is in the second sense that the word "elitist" has to be understood. Certainly, Spinoza was not an "elitist" in this sense, since he strove to open up the way to understanding of oneself, Nature, and God, to all. Moreover, he believed that everybody has the innate capability to become free. Enlightenment and freedom begins, for Spinoza, with the person, while for Marx, it was a matter of collective freedom preceding individual liberation.

4. The Diversity of Human Needs

The awareness of a need makes its realization possible. Thus, the awareness of freedom is a precondition for being free, and similarly with the entire cluster of needs that condition the freedom of human beings. In order for us to realize our intellectual, aesthetic, moral, and emotional needs, we must first be aware of them. The awareness of physical needs is immediate and direct. This makes their fulfillment prior to all other needs. The fulfillment of physical and material needs mediates the fulfillment of all the higher level needs. If there is an exaggerated preoccupation with the physical needs, the other cultural and spiritual needs will never come to be mediated into the individual's consciousness. The question of need awareness (in the higher regions of our needs) is fundamental. The very possibility of their fulfillment depends on this. In addition, people may have distorted notions about these higher level needs, even to the extent that they are aware of them. For example, people may underrate or overrate their intellectual potential. They may aspire to an intellectual achievement that does not reflect their true inner creative and free needs. To know our potential in the sphere of our intellect or mental capability is not simply a matter of a given awareness of ourselves. It involves the recognition and the knowledge of our inner self, our true interests, inclinations, our mental practices and habits, such as thinking, interpreting, reading, absorbing, comprehending, integrating, and concentrating. Most of all, it requires utmost self-honesty in our endeavor to overcome self-deception. The danger of self-deception and exaggerated self-perception is forever present. This is always the case, when need awareness arises from confused ideas about ourselves, and when it is propelled by external factors. Thus, the source of such needs may be the desire to impress others with our intelligence, goodness of heart, or any other desirable quality. The origin of such needs can usually be traced back to some adverse outside influences, such as family and other experiences during childhood, which have become implanted in the person's unconscious. To this extent, they are like passions, which rule and dominate the person. When the person is carried away by such higher level needs that are in truth passions, his or her mind is passive. The endeavor to carry them out will be compulsive, such as the compulsive need to write, to create, or to be artistic. These exaggerated needs will most often bring frustration, pain, and mediocre performance in their wake. Once we are able to confront such phantom (pseudo-creative and pseudo-spiritual) needs, there is a good possibility that we will be able to identify the extraneous origin of these needs and the fixed hold that they exercise on us. By reflecting on their true nature and the external causes behind them, our mind will be activated, and we may become free of their fixed hold over us. By this free thought and activity, the very same needs may now become free needs, activated from within. These needs will be clearly understood and therefore cease to be compulsive needs. The freedom associated with the fulfillment of free needs brings immense joy to the person, while the attempt to meet false, compulsive needs, brings only pain and sorrow to the individual. On top of this, compulsive needs can never really be satisfied.

The same holds true for all the other spheres of our existence. In the ethical sphere, the right conduct has to emanate from within the person. It has to be a free decision or free choice rather than a conventionally determined one, that is forced from without. The latter is part of a confused idea of morality. Such confusion extends itself to the whole conventional morality including Judeo-Christian ethics. The religious and conventional ethics is an ethics of conduct instead of an ethics of being. It pertains to the relation of the individual to the other, such as, the Golden Rule, or the Categorical Imperative. It does not deal with the relation of the individual to himself or herself in freedom. But an ethics that does not address itself to the inner freedom of human beings and stresses instead, their behavior toward others, is at best a superficial ethics, and eventually a vulgar one. Such an ethics may make us comply with rules of conduct reinforced with the fear of punishment (by God or the authorities), but it will never succeed in making us truly ethical from within. Only when we free ourselves from the bondage of conventional morality, can we really rise to the true morality based on inner freedom and on the clear and distinct understanding of ourselves and others. In a community of free people, the notion of good and bad, the ethical conduct toward each other, becomes entirely superfluous and indeed, comical. The actions of free people come from within. Their minds are activated and joyful. They view themselves and each other with the dignity of a person who understands God, eternity, and the transitoriness of the mode's durational existence. For such a person, the mere idea of taking advantage of another, of injuring or discriminating against another, is an alien idea. Quite the opposite, the person will experience joy every time he or she can lend a helping hand to another in need. The joy is the inner expression of a free act. Now we can see why Spinoza named his most important book *Ethics*, without even once mentioning this word in the entire text.

Notes

1. On this, see Jon Wetlesen, *The Sage and the Way*. Assen, Netherlands: Van Gorcum, 1979. p.103.
2. Abraham Maslow, *Motivation and Personality*, New York: Harper & Row, 1970.
3. Karl Marx, *Capital*, Vol.1, New York: International Publishers, 1973. p.72.
4. Karl Marx, *Economic and Philosophic Manuscripts of 1844*, New York: International Publishers, p.147.
5. Ibid.
6. Maslow, *Motivation and Personality*.

CHAPTER 8
A FREE INTERPRETATION OF SPINOZA'S NOTION OF EXISTENTIAL ESSENCE: THE STRIVING FOR CREATIVE SELF-EXPRESSION

"The human nature, as well as every other type of being has built into it the specific norm of its own self realization or self preservation".[1]

I. CREATIVE SELF- EXPRESSION

1. The Uniqueness of the Individual

The uniqueness of the individual strives to express itself. Each one has its own norm for self-realization. It forms the basis for its creativity. Creativity is conditioned by the individual's willingness and ability to be true to himself and to accept himself. Each path in life and each existence is uniquely our own.

To live creatively is to express my individuality in whatever I do. I relate to my family, my work, and the world around me, from the center of my being. I am the true cause of my actions and beliefs. My mind is thereby active, and my conduct is determined by reason instead of impulse or compulsion.

To the extent that I am free to express my true self, I am creative. The freedom to be, is the freedom to be myself, free from internal impediments. It is also the freedom to become the unique person that I am, without external barriers placed on my potentially full development. Since I can never be someone else (not me), I can only be free in being myself. Conversely, to the extent that I am consciously or unconsciously trying to be what I am not, I cannot be free. All freedom is by necessity based on self-acceptance and self-knowledge. Creative living extends to all areas of life. It requires full involvement in the activity at hand. The encounter of another will be exhilarating to the extent that it stimulates self-expression. (Similarly with any other activity.)

To read creatively means to internalize and integrate the essential ideas contained in the reading. This requires critical reflection and relating those ideas to my experiences. The newly acquired knowledge becomes itself a new experience. It becomes truly my own. It is being appropriated and subjectivized. I can use it in new learning.

To the extent that I am free to be myself in every involvement that I have (in my work, in my dealings with others, in my interaction with friends and family, in my participation in the community), I express myself creatively in life. Creativity is thus linked to freedom. The ultimate meaning of both creativity and freedom is the freedom to be. Creativity is not confined to genius or to any especially privileged person. Just as genius expresses his uniqueness in whatever he does, so can each person live creatively, if he allows himself to be himself. We can say with Spinoza, that this means to live our life guided by reason. This is also the innermost secret of happiness, since every transition from the not self to the self, that is , from a lower to a higher level of reality (or perfection) brings with it a feeling of joy (EIII, 11, Note).

When life evolves around appearances, man becomes not an end in himself but a means towards something outside him. When appearance is the primary mode of life, self-estrangement   sets in. The person's potentially creative uniqueness is repressed and made subservient to outside "success." We seek to impress others not by what we are (our inner quality of character), but by what we have, namely, by externals such as money, wealth, power, and fame. Underlying all of this is the hunger to be acknowledged and recognized. But such acknowledgment is not recognition of the true person. The need to live up to an image becomes burdensome in the end. Life gets to be reduced to an alienated and functional existence that cannot bring inner peace to the person.

In order to be free, I must look at my innermost nature objectively and realistically. I must unravel those subconscious forces that prevent me from seeing myself objectively and rationally, instead of compulsively and irrationally. Thus I get to the essence of myself.

2. The Meaning of Essence

Spinoza uses the term "essence" in different ways. He defines "the actual essence of a thing" as the power of a thing to persist in its own being (EIII, 9, Schol.). This singular essence has two dimensions, an eternal one and a temporal one. Reason constitutes man's eternal essence. "It is in the nature of reason to perceive things under a certain form of eternity" (EII, 44, Corrol.). The temporal essence of man is the essence of his durational existence. Man's eternal essence is a free cause, it is determined from within (EI, Def. 7). The temporal essence of man is determined from within and from without, that is, "by a fixed and determinate method of existence or action" (ibid.). It is not a free but a necessary cause, for it is codetermined from without. In a more fundamental sense, Spinoza uses the term essence as "that without which the thing could neither be nor be conceived." In this sense, God is the essence of all things.

In what follows, I limit myself to Spinoza's temporal meaning of the human essence. I will call it the existential essence of the person or the essence of the person's existence. Each life has its own essence. Each life has to be lived individually and uniquely. Existence is strictly my own. To know my essence is to know my "telos". My "telos" represents my possibilities that strive to realize themselves. It is the striving (*conatus* or desire) to fulfill my nature. Aristotle's natural teleology and Spinoza's *conatus* express the same idea of nature's striving to fulfill itself.

We can however, through our consciousness, interfere with our natural or God given "telos". Through ignorance or false consciousness, we can fail to know our true essence. To know my true "telos" is to know the basic forces, capabilities, and limitations, that make up the unique person that I am. For Spinoza, lasting happiness can ultimately be attained only in the knowledge of God. Each of us however, must travel this road by ourselves. We can by no means be assured that we will get to its ultimate destination. While the final destination is the same for all, each existence is unique and individual. Each of us must come to know God in our individual way. On our way to our final destination, on our journey toward the state of lasting blessedness, we need to accommodate ourselves to less perfect states, where not only happiness is at stake, but where we may be besieged with self-doubt, adversity, and weakness. The problem of finding the essence of our existence pertains not to ultimate salvation, but to the way toward it. It is the problem of how to deal with existential adversity. We need to discover our true self for the sake of that. We need to know our unique being, our sameness and difference from others. We need to know our basic drives and needs, the fulfillment of which will give us a measure of happiness, while at the same time pointing the way to ultimate salvation and blessedness. Even if we fail to reach that ultimate destination, we will have lived our life according to our laws, the laws of our nature.

3. My Own Telos

I am my own telos. I have to discover it within me. I have to know the laws of my nature. My telos is to be true to myself. That is what Spinoza did when he was reflecting on the direction to give to his life. The direction is the telos. Life without direction can not be free or meaningful. To be myself is to conquer all fear in me. I can be without fear because to be afraid of myself is absurd. I can only be afraid of others, that is, of the image of myself. I can worry about what others think about me, but not of what I think about myself. What I think of myself I can only try to understand. Through understanding, I can remove all fear that is within me. If I allow myself to be myself, I can live freely and joyfully. I can be spontaneous and creative.

The laws of our nature are leitmotifs that accompany us throughout life. When we uphold them we feel happy. When we do not uphold them, either through ignorance or circumstance, we cannot feel happy. This is true even if we experience outward success. Therefore we have to become aware of our leitmotifs. They have to be brought into awareness and dealt with consciously. These leitmotifs are our basic drives and needs. We can readily give examples of these strivings: Strivings for love (to give and receive love), for recognition, for openness in friendship, for justice, etc. These strivings and their realization are the *raison d'etre* of our innermost being. When they are left unexpressed and unconscious, they will become exaggerated, idealized, and rigidified. This will prevent us from seeing them realistically, foreclosing the possibility of their realization. We will not be able to attain existential well- being.

Existential well-being can only be achieved through the re-establishing of personal harmony with our life's essence. The possibility of doing this exists throughout our entire lifetime. At whatever stage in life we realize our essence, and the need to uphold it rather than to compromise it, we achieve a measure of existential freedom, transcendence, and inner peace. This refusal to compromise our true nature is the true source of happiness. The ability to know ourselves realistically rather than through suppressed phantasy brings with it the condition for self-fulfillment and the power to realize it. Past failures, when evaluated with objective awareness, turn into past experience and become a source of self-understanding as well as an opportunity for new learning. That is what "to live in reality" means. It means to avoid the double traps of delusion and self-defeatism. It means not to give in to our physical and emotional losses that tax our hope, courage, vitality, and spirit. To live in reality means to recognize the potential imbued in this reality and to act on it.

This acting from within ourselves is the ultimate meaning of freedom. We begin to live our possibility and our potentiality. Although we do not not know our potentiality with any degree of precision, we are usually aware of its broad limits. We work within these limits and the work itself has the effect of ever-widening these limits. In other words, potentiality develops through use. Human potentiality should be viewed as a range with variable scope. It is not a final boundary line that cannot be crossed. We do not know with any degree of certainty the limits to our potentiality. "However, no one has hitherto laid down the limits to the power of the body" (EII, 2, Note), and correspondingly, to the power of the mind. No one has yet exhausted the possibilities imbued in reason. God is infinite reason, and man shares in God by exploiting the possibilities given to us by reason.

4. Human Potentiality

We can ascertain our potentiality only to the extent that we exercise our abilities in practice. We can always push forward toward the limits of our potentiality, but the full realization of our potential will necessarily remain beyond our reach. Each area of life has its potentiality. Physical, moral, and spiritual strength, intellectual vigor, aesthetic sensitivity, all these represent different potentialities for different people. These potentialities do not necesarily synchronize with each other. The notion of human potentiality is complex. We verify our potentiality through our deeds and through the realization of those pursuits that reflect our true inner self.

Individual uniqueness, that is, each life's essence, is at bottom unexplainable. It is the divine spark that represents this individual uniqueness. The divine, creative essence is imbued in the person's uniqueness. It is divine because it is associated with nature's creation (*Natura naturans*). The uniqueness of each mode is established in EI, 28: "Every individual thing....cannot exist or be conditioned to act, unless it be conditioned for existence and action by a cause other than itself...., and so on to infinity." If there was a break in the infinite series of causes that conditioned my existence, then I would not be the individual (mode) that I am. I would still exist as a modal essence, a non-existent mode. This modal essence would be a *res physica*, underlying the same set of efficient causes as existing modes.[2] "God is the efficient cause not only of the existence of things, but also of their essence"(EI, 25). All modal essences are subject to and explainable by the series of causes in nature. Thus, "our mind is not, like our body, subject to the vicissitudes of circumstance....all the clear and distinct perceptions which we form, can only arise from other clear and distinct perceptions, which are in us:" (Letter 42 to I. Bresser). Purely fictitious ideas are divorced from the series of causes in nature. They have no modal essences.

Non-existent modes as modal essences are at the base of human creativity. Creative or non-representational imagination embraces these essences. In the realm of thought, we are free to form true ideas and in this we come closer to God. The uniqueness of each individual expresses itself in his or her ability to form and comprehend true ideas. As part of nature, God's creating and created powers, *Natura naturans* and *Natura naturata*, are within us. Our creativity is connected to nature's creation, "we depend in such a way on that which is the most perfect of all, that we also are as part of the whole, that is of him; and, so to say, bring to it also our share toward elaboration of so many aptly ordered and perfect works as are dependent thereon."[3]

However, this divine spark given to us by birthright can too easily be extinguished, because we are not God. We are therefore weak. Our creativity is fragile and brittle. It can easily be killed through lack of nurture and by an injurious, indifferent, and alienating social environment. We need to be recognized by other human beings in order to strive and create. Pressures to defeat our creativity and potentiality lurk everywhere. We can resist them or give in to them. These pressures build around us from our earliest beginnings. If we give in to these pressures, we let our creative uniqueness atrophy by failing to build on it and to develop it. Eventually we will lose our creativity altogether and we will no longer be aware of it. This can happen quite early in life.

Creativity is either nurtured or destroyed. But we can stop and reverse direction at any stage of our life. Through becoming aware of ourselves, we can choose not to give in to the path of temptation. We can choose to assert ourselves over our environment and pursue our true essence. We may choose freedom over unfreedom. This choice is always available to us. Spinoza's notion of freedom is not the Kantian freedom in the nouminal world defined as "the faculty of starting an event spontaneously"[4] whereby man as a being of reason is free to follow the Categorical Imperative. Neither is it the Sartrean notion of freedom whereby we are free to choose our character and our values. In Sartre, man is always free to choose how to react to his "facticity". "I am absolutely free and absolutely responsible for my situation."[5] For Spinoza, freedom is a possibility. It is not absolute. We can be more free or less free. We can enlarge the realm of freedom by increasing our comprehension of ourselves and of nature. And this is Spinoza's most powerful message. The power of the message lies in the possibility of its attainment. We are capable of understanding ourselves and knowing God. Since reason is given to us, we can use it to understand ourselves, to know ourselves and be free.

5. The Freedom To Be Ourselves

This freedom to be ourselves is what we have called the "law of our being." It is that mystery of our self that permits the joy of life to express and unfold itself in its positive, pure, and unrestrained form. It is that irreducible quality that ultimately sustains the individual in the face of defeats, disappointments and frustrations. It is that hidden power which gives him reason and strength to go on with his life's journey. The law of our being is that irreducible quality that serves us as a last source of strength and support when everything else has been put under existential questioning and doubt. It reawakens in us the belief in life, and the conviction that life itself is never without meaning. Life is always meaningful and inherently joyful. Spinoza's active virtue is enjoyment, ..."I enjoy life, and try to spend it not in sorrow and sighing, but in peace, joy and cheerfulnesss, ascending from time to time a step higher" (Letter 34 to Blyenbergh). Joy is the affirmation of life. Life in its pure form is always joyful. This can be seen in the infant. When the infant's essential needs (love and nurture) are satisfied, he is a bundle of joy. The manifold expressions of aliveness (heightened sensations, wonder, imagination, action, intense concentration and work, spontaneity,) are always experienced as joy. The joy of life need not necessarily express itself in outward movement, ecstasy or activity. Its inward manifestation can be felt with the same intensity. This inward feeling *(beatudo)* is the experience of joy as the total relaxation of body and mind in the intellectual love of God.

6. The Essence of Life

If there is a way to capture the meaning of the essence of life, I would say, that the essence of a person's life is to enrich all life through his own life. "the sum of the divine law (which....has been divinely inscribed on our hearts), and its chief precept is, to love God as the highest good: not, indeed, from the fear of any punishment, for love cannot spring from fear; nor the love of anything which we desire for our own delight, for then we should love not God, but the object of our desire" (Letter 59 to Isaac Orobio). Happiness demands that each individual makes a contribution to all life, to all humanity. A selfish life, a life lived for oneself, can never be a happy one, "the life of man is not a service for wages: what is called happiness is not the reward for virtue but virtue itself."[6] The same is expressed by the Jewish Talmud, in the Sayings of the Fathers: If I am not for myself who is for me? And when I am only for myself what am I? And if not now, when?[7] Only when our life is directed to something larger than ourselves (to our common humanity), will our essence engulf our being and our experience will be filled with it. Our experience will express the joy and bliss of creation. This is the meaning of Spinoza's definition of the human essence as self-preservation and self-elevation. Self-elevation cannot be divorced from self-preservation. "Nothing can be in more harmony with the nature of any given thing than other individuals of the same species; therefore for man in the preservation of his being and the enjoyment of the rational life there is nothing more useful than his fellow man who is led by reason" (EIV, App. 9). "Yet minds are not conquered by force, but by love and high-mindednesss"(EIV, App. 11).

The expression of this individual essence is not limited to any single sphere of our existence. It is nevertheless my central premise, that our work, broadly defined, forms the basis for the unfolding of our creativity in all other areas of our life. Thus, work (projects) is central to human well being and happiness. To the extent that I express my true self in my actions, in my deeds and in my work, I develop, grow, learn, and improve. Work becomes enjoyable and we perform it with relative ease and grace. We cease to strive for perfection in our endeavors. We strive only for improvement and competence. Thus, we free ourselves from any compulsion within the innumerable obligations, responsibilities and life's interdependencies. We become truly independent in our spirit.

All other expressions of our life are contingent on their broad conformity with the basic direction given by our life's essence. Life's activities will conform to and express life's essence. They cannot deny it. "So long as we are not assailed by emotions contrary to our nature, we have the power of arranging and associating the modifications of our body according to the intellectual order"(EV, 10). A denial of the basic law of our nature brings with it a retardation of our life forces, whereas a sense of consistency with it, enhances all life forces within us. I can feel my essence through its effect on my existence. If we do something that corresponds to our essential being, all exhilarating effects take place. Similarly, when we feel exhilarated by our activity in conformity with the rational order, we know that we have acted in accordance with our true essence. For example, for a person whose life has been ruled by a deep sense of justice, any active expression of it will exhilarate and uplift the person. On the other hand, a withdrawal into an uninvolved life would bring about a deterioration of the person's life forces.

7. The Question of Good and Evil

We have come back to the problem of good and evil. If the potentiality inherent in us is bent on destruction, and if it is turned against ourselves, against others, or against humanity, can we still refer to it as the divine spark given to us by nature? Schelling argues affirmatively. He says, that evil is also in God.[8] The question remains, whether we can fulfill our essence by doing evil. Is the demonic and destructive potential rooted in us just as the life-giving and life-enriching potential is? Or does the one deny the validity of the other?

Let us see how Spinoza deals with this problem of evil:

"it follows solely from the perfection of God, that God never can decree, or never could have decreed anything but what is; that God did not exist before his decrees, and would not exist without them" (EI, 33, Note.). We cannot assign qualities or judgments, such as good, bad, vice, and evil, to God. All determination is negation (Letter 50 to Jelles). Notions of good and bad, vice or virtue, benevolence or evil, have no relevance to God.

But they certainly are relevant to man. With respect to man, Spinoza defines good and bad, (or good and evil), in terms of what enhances our power to act. Thus, sadness is bad, joy is good (EIV, 41). Everything that diminishes our power of acting (sadness, frustration, hatred,) is bad. That includes any passive emotion, such as, pity, hope, remorse, and guilt. What has the contrary effect, what enhances our power to act, is good. What is useful to us is good. What is harmful (decreases our power to act) is bad.

This requires a specific interpretation. What Spinoza means by "the power to act" is the mind's power to act on the basis of reason and not on the basis of emotion. It is essentially the power to understand ourselves and the power to know God. Such power cannot be turned against another. That would be substituting the power of the gun, (or force in all its concomitant forms, such as, wealth, tyranny, domination, and political power) for the power of the mind. This is not what Spinoza meant by equating the useful with the good and the harmful with evil. Moreover, if good is what enhances our power of acting while evil is what diminishes those powers, it necessarily follows, that what is good holds for all people without any discrimination between them. All people participate in God's essence (reason), and God is inmmanent in all of us. Evil is what is turned against other people, or against humanity. "It is part of the wise man....to make use of that what comes in our way and to enjoy it as much as possible....without injury to his neighbor" (EIV, 45, Note). Thus, to injure our neighbor is to do evil. There is nevertheless an inconsistency built in to the equation of good with the power of reason. This equation holds only to the extent that we are free. It does not fully hold for persons, even when they are on their way to becoming free, and it certainly does not hold for the individual who is not free. Since most of humanity is in a state of unfreedom, the equating of good with power to act, is likely to be misunderstood, misrepresented, and misapplied.

8. The Existential Question of Life's Meaning

The question of meaning arises when our life revolves around mechanical, repetitive routines. If my life has become a series of repetitive chores, what is the meaning of it? Do these chores constitute my life, or is there anything more to it? Are the life-enabling daily operations the purpose of my living or are they the means to my living? And, if it is the latter, then what is the larger purpose of my life, a life to which so much of my energies are used in order to sustain it? Since physical existence cannot be its own purpose (not by bread alone does a person live), the larger purpose gives meaning to life. I have to search for this larger purpose and thereby assign meaning to my existence. If I have not understood the larger meaning of my existence, I will be facing existential dread, Angst, (anguish, or anxiety), unless I become an unthinking or insensitive creature. Thus, we come back to our previous proposition that life can only have meaning if it is lived for the sake of some larger purpose than itself. All life-sustaining chores become meaningful if they serve to sustain a life with meaning (a life that points to some larger purpose than itself.) This includes all the material or physical pleasures and enjoyments. These enjoyments by themselves cannot be the purpose of life. I do not and cannot exist for the sake of sensual, aesthetic, or material pleasures. Such pleasures are refinements of life, but not purposes. On their own, they lack meaning. Their meaning is derivative from a life that has meaning. Without a meaningful life, they will not even be experienced as pleasures. Where do I look for meaning? I will now deviate from Spinoza's fundamental meaning of life in the knowledge of God, and will work it out

132

from a more gradualist, and more common perspective, which will eventually lead to Spinoza's fundamental insight.

The answer to the problem of meaning is, that we can find meaning everywhere, in all areas of our existence (work, family, friends, nature, and solitude). The meaning derives from self- knowledge. It comes to me when I recognize myself as the person that I am. Only then will others also recognize me as the person that I am. And recognition is at the root of existence. I confer meaning on my existence when I know and understand myself in my work, in my love, in my family, in my friendships, and in all areas of my life. This self-understanding will be reflected in the recognition by others. The genuineness of my existence will be responded to by others in their recognition of me as the person that I am. The problem is circular. To be recognized for what I am, I must first be who I am: I must be the genuine self. To be genuine is a precondition for being recognized. Recognition is essential for existing, it is a fundamental human need. It adds strength and meaning to our life. We find worth in our actions and in our being and we are appreciated for being who we are. Since no one lives in solitude, appreciative feedback, support and recognition are indispensable for human happiness. We need friends and a supportive environment on our way to freedom. This is easier said than done. Our environment is not usually structured to help us grow and become more free. Here we turn to Spinoza to point the way.

Spinoza was the first real existentialist. He specifically dealt with problems of human existence. For him, meaning is built-in to a life that is free, and to a life that aspires to be free. He points toward a life of joy, inner directedness, and the enhancement of our active powers. Under the guide of reason, a freedom based on understanding means reaching higher levels of perfection and reality. Such transitions to enhanced self-understanding and reason, which are equivalent to reaching higher levels of reality and perfection, express themselves as joy. Meaning is intrinsic to a life that is free and to one that aspires to be free. Only when we spend our life in a negative frame of mind, when we are afflicted with negative emotions of pain, fear, self-pity, self-doubt, or hate, does the existential question of meaning arise. The question is based on ignorance. All negative emotions stem from the ignorance of their extraneous causes. Positive emotions are based on the knowledge of their true causes.

Existence, however, is more complicated than that. It is not always or for the most part joyful. It exhibits emotional ups and downs, successes and failures, achievements and reversals, conflict and resolution, and so on. Spinoza provides a way of dealing with existential conflict and with the downside of life. Here the striving of the person to become free takes on significance. This struggle for freedom, specifically involves the activation of our mind and the use of our inherently human powers of reason and understanding. Only this way, can we turn the downside into the upside, the negative into the positive, the pain into pleasure. Meaning comes as a necessary complement of this struggle for our freedom. We get meaning through the joy of living, doing, acting, feeling, loving, and giving. All of this is clearly personal and individual. No one exists for me, and there is no substitute for my existing. Yet, while no one can feel my pain (at least not in the way I feel it), others will more readily identify with my joy. While suffering is solitary, joy radiates to the outside.

Especially in times of crisis we are disposed to make the leap from meaninglessness to meaning, from a meaningless existence to the search for a meaningful life, from an unquestioning attitude to a questioning attitude. That road toward meaning goes through our selves.

Spinoza has shown us a way to overcome weakness and anxiety that arises from a feeling of meaninglessness and impotency. We can increase our powers of acting through taking command of ourselves instead of allowing ourselves to be ruled by our passsions. Our passions always derive from external causes. Whenever I am the true cause of my acting, I am self- directing and free. As a result, I will always feel joy. When I feel joy, I am using my inner powers and resources for productive pursuits, I am activating the powers of my mind and my body. This activation of our powers of mind and body is the source of human happiness. A productive orientation in life is at the center of happiness both for Spinoza and Aristotle. For, "Happiness....is the end of action" (Aristotle, Metaphysics, 1097 b 22).

This striving for wholeness, for the unfolding of the possibilities imbued in my potential along with the consciousness of these possibilities, constitutes the essence of the human being. It is ultimately a striving to be free. Without such striving, that is, without my essence, I feel fragmented, alienated, lonely, and depersonalized. I feel less human. My life needs to be centered on the possibilities that are imbued in me. My life needs to be centered on some larger task instead of being centered on me. If my life evolves only around me, it will lack meaning. If it is centered outside of me (on my possibilities for work, love, joy, excitement, wonder,) it will lend meaning to my existence. I need to be creative. I need to unite with nature's creative force. I am part of *Natura naturans*. I strive to be what I am and to be recognized as such. I strive to be recognized for the work that I am doing, and for the person that I am. In this connenction, Hegel's master-slave dialectic was nothing but the fight for mutual recognition.

Spinoza pointed the way to self-discovery and to self-understanding. He has shown us the way to wholeness and freedom. He has given us the key to unlock the darker recesses of our nature and free their potential energy for joyous and productive pursuits. He has shown us the right way to live. This is why he has called his major work "Ethics".

Humanity will forever strive for freedom and independence. Let me now briefly recapitulate the meaning of freedom:

To become more free, means:

To be able to discriminate between the more important and the less important on a corresponding scale of values and priorities;

To avoid self-deception and pretense;

To live and realize our values;

To grasp and utilize the opportunities that life offers;

To develop our inner resources and become stronger;

To grow in our relation with others through the practice of patience, understanding, and active listening;

To recognize and accept my limitations and those of others around me;

To take seriously my responsibilities as a citizen and a member of my community;

To actively involve myself in building a society guided by reason, justice, and moral values;

To better understand myself and the society I live in;

To balance the present with the future through my understanding of the past;

To experience harmony, peace, serenity, inner joy and enthusiasm of being alive.

Our existence will always necessitate a compromise between our aspirations and their fulfillment. The need to compromise does not negate the need to be true to ourselves (our essence). The question is whether the necessary compromises in life (that of our existence), will be made within or outside of our true essence. The question is whether we will uphold our integrity amid the vagaries of life. This means that whatever a person does, whatever action we take or decision we make, the spring of such action should always lie within ourselves and not outside ourselves. Every person must ultimately assume full responsibility for his or her actions and for his or her existence.

We may observe our existence and distill its essence. Often the same few themes keep recurring throughout the individual's life, in totally different situations. Recurring patterns of existence may be positive or negative. They may promote or hinder the person's growth to freedom. However, growth inhibiting patterns of behavior are at odds with our true essence. Only life-enhancing patterns of existence are compatible with the individual's true essence. This is a fundamental lesson that Spinoza teaches us.

9. The Problem of Practice

The problem of practice involves the coordination and the fusion of thought with action.[9] The failure or the postponement to fuse action with thought is the most troublesome aspect of the person's existence. If we overestimate our expectations and our capabilities, then we will not be able to realize them. As a result, action will lag behind thought, and wishful thinking will replace reality. This will lead to inner conflict. The conflict calls for resolution. The resolution involves a realistic appreciation of our existence.

To resolve this existential conflict, we may start with our work. To what extent am I interested in my work? Do I find creative outlets in my work? Or, does my work merely serve my survival needs? If it is the latter, what are my possibilities to change the situation? Can I make my work more rewarding and creative? If such possibilities are foreclosed, then I will have to find and develop other interests or activities in addition to my regular work experience.

The point is, that we must cultivate areas of potential creativity. A person's need of finding avenues for creative self- expression in work (broadly defined as projects), is as real, as the need to provide for material welfare. Only through our work, (projects) do we get to know ourselves. Work is the basis of life. It ties the individual to society. It legitimizes our existence. It is the fundamental source of self-esteem, social standing, and inner well-being. It is the principal source of experience, growth, and learning. Optimally, it should serve as an outlet for our creative energies.

We need to connect with others through our work. That is how work is sustained, nourished, renewed, energized, and enjoyed. A genuine interest in our work would almost automatically create a social environment that transcends its formal structures. This is so because all work is social in nature, it requires the interaction of many people.

However, our society does not allow for the average person the possibility of self-fulfillment through work. Industrial efficiency is based on market-determined laws of exchange and not on people's higher level needs. Work alienation is the general malaise of our industrial system. Alienation whose origin lies at the work place, becomes pervasive throughout all areas of our social life.

If a person's work is looked upon as a necessary evil rather than as a source for creative self-fulfillment, than loneliness is an inevitable result. Loneliness and alienation are outward manifestations of people's lack of interest in their work. Lack of genuine and creative interest in their work deprives people of their inner bonds between them (shared work experiences and interests). Work is thus deprived of its innermost satisfaction as a source of inner joy that comes from sharing, giving and communicating with one another freely and spontaneously. The lack of involvement with one's work deprives the individual of a natural center of gravity from which an entire spectrum of other interests may emanate. Again, this leads to loneliness and alienation.

People may protect themselves from the system and from the general condition of work alienation that permeates our society, by exploring ways of improving the conditions of their work or by cultivating other interests, either as hobbies, or by turning these new interests into a condition for their material existence. It is imperative that we like ourselves at work and that we like the work that we are doing. If people cannot express themselves and their creativity in their work, they need to find other avenues for self-expression.

All creativity seeks expression. If it is denied the opportunity to self-express, it will be suppressed and eventually lost to the person. Creative self-expression needs to be cultivated throughout our entire life-time. The work of the artist may serve as a case in point. The artists' life, their creativity and their personhood are united through their work. That many unknown artists choose to live on a level of minimum physical comfort in order to satisfy their creative needs testifies to the strength of such needs among those whose potential creativity has not been lost early in life.

10. Loneliness and Alienation in the Social Sphere

The lack of involvement or real interest in our work expresses itself in the social sphere as a lack of involvement with each other, or as indifference toward each other. People are not sharing each other's joys and sorrows even if they seem concerned on the surface. People talk to each other without reaching each other. They are not inclined to give out of an inner need for giving, without expecting anything in return. Since nobody is willing to give without ascertaining what he or she is getting, real reaching out to people becomes impossible. The inability to communicate on a human level, involving reason and feeling, is nothing but an extension of market relations of exchange into the sphere of social relations. This objectification and reification of human relations deadens the spirit that animates the living individual. Human interactions become spiritless, joyless, without involvement, without compassion, and ultimately without meaning. Individuals gradually lose their ability to feel, to introspect, and to look into others. They lose their human sensitivity. They become mechanical in their reactions. Their intelligence develops in the direction of a computing machine that operates with maximum efficiency but lacks independent judgment and cannot think.

When exchange value and exchange relations intrude into the realm of the social sphere, people lose inner excitement and become apathetic. Apathy may be defined as a lack of involvement plus self-centeredness. Apathetic individuals are unenthusiastic, not trusting, unbelieving, and uninvolved. The root cause of apathy is lack of hope, faith, and love. Apathy then turns into cynicism. People become apathetic when they are unable to deal with their inner contradictions and conflicts. As a result, life is reduced to stagnation and mere existing. People become unresponsive to the needs of others, as seen in everyday life. For example, apathetic teachers are unresponsive to the needs of their students, and apathetic doctors are unresponsive to the needs of their patients. Apathetic people are not involved in their work. Such people ultimately face the choice between spiritual death and moral rebellion.

138

Another consequence of a society dominated by machine technology is the spread of boredom. Along with the increased access and the availability of leisure time, is the simultaneous inability of the individual to enjoy and utilize his or her leisure for rewarding and stimulating avenues for personal growth. The very system (the advanced machine-dominated industrial system) that made leisure available, denies the people in a thousand different, subtle and not so subtle ways, the means to a self-fulfilling enjoyment of their leisure time. Boredom spreads and with it, the need for thrills as a way to counteract it and escape from it. Thus, people travel compulsively, and watch television endlessly. That only aggravates the problem. It leads to spiritual and mental retardation, and perhaps to crime.

Whole new industries have come up to cater to leisure activities. This commercialization of leisure increases the profitability of the system, while at the same time it serves as a prop to the system. The dulling of the senses and the recession of the personality through the submission to the commercialization of leisure is another manifestation of the anonymous control by the system of the people.

11. The Problem of Practice Redefined

In EIV, 21 Spinoza identifies existence with action. Only the person who acts "actually exists." The failure to fuse or to follow up thought with action intensifies the contradiction between commitment and belief. It thereby results in a lack of freedom. It leads to a nagging thought of failing to live up to our beliefs. This spells inner conflict and tension. The inner conflict calls for resolution. The most obvious place to start to resolve this conflict involves our work or projects. How do I make my work more meaningful to me? The resolution of the conflict calls for a realistic appreciation of my work options and of my independent or personal projects. My projects need be made precise, concrete, and realistic. I must avoid projects that I am unable to define clearly, or that are beyond my capacity to carry out. I must avoid faulty design, exaggerated plans, or inadequate preparation. I should not be blinded by the need to do something significant, great, or extraordinary. These are delusions, false plans, and pitfalls. They are compulsions and passions that hinder my power to act. We must conquer the hidden enemies that lurk in the background in the form of a compulsive neurotic need for greatness or significance. We should overcome the need to make an impact or a contribution to real social change through our projects. We free ourselves from these inhibiting passions by becoming aware of their true nature. They all stem from extraneous causes. We need to realize that enjoyable work (projects that express our true essence) is its own reward. This has long been known by the ancient Hindus. It is the main message that the Bhagavad Gita contains.

Thus, there is no need to prove "my greatness," or my "exceptional qualities" through my work projects. (Such work is not internally directed, and therefore, it is not free.) I need not be "great" or "extraordinary" to be accepted and respected. Respect comes in the first instance from self-respect. Self-respect means to be true to myself. Self-acceptance, is the basis for self- respect, which in turn is the basis for respect by others. What I can do (great projects,) has nothing to do with what I am (the dignity of my being). I need not justify my being by my achievements. Neither need it be justified by "social significance" or by my contribution to a better world. My contribution to a better world is the result of my living in accordance with my human essence and not its condition. Thus, to live the right way, in accordance with my basic nature, is first of all to be free to be myself and not aspire to things that are external to my nature (social approbation). It means not to be compelled to do good, or to be somebody special, or to carry out a mission dictated by my "calling." These are all the wrong reasons for my practice. They are acts of unfreedom rather than of freedom.

Freedom requires a sense of direction. The sum total of an individual's actions need conform to some consistent pattern expressing purpose. This lends structure and movement to a person's existence. A person is free to act in accordance with his or her basic purpose and be consistent with it. An individual's life is no longer arbitrary or haphazard. A life that conforms to some overall inner design gives strength to the person. Without a sense of direction, freedom is not possible. A lack of direction leads to a diffusion of energy and to random living that is often mistaken for living in the present.

II. WHAT DOES IT MEAN TO LIVE IN THE PRESENT?

1. Direction, Movement, Vision and Purpose

Living in the present requires direction, movement, vision, and purpose. Without them, living in the present becomes living for the present, which may well turn out to be living for the moment, or an empty life. Therefore, to live fully in the present, means: to live in accordance with my true essence, to resolve inner conflicts, to be involved with my work, to be productive and creative, to use my time effectively, to carry out my responsibilities to my fellow human beings, to my family, and to myself. I gain an overall sense of active well- being.

When conflicts arise, at work, in the family, or within myself, and when I am pulled in different directions all at once, such conflicts need to be dealt with, in the present. I cannot go on living with lingering, unresolved conflicts. I need to be aware of them and deal with them in a manner that would lead to their realistic resolution. This involves the awareness of the true nature of the conflict, the constraints imposed by the reality of my situation, the recognition of the factors that are subject to personal discretion and control, and above all, the need to act under the guidance of reason. A rational resolution of the conflict will necessarily reflect my concern for personal and social welfare, the recognition and the awareness of the need to face life contingencies, the need for personal movement and growth, the need to benefit and learn from my experiences. Living in the present cannot be divorced from the direction of my life, that is, from the future. What living in the present does not mean is, living in the past. I cannot dwell on past glories, or have remorse and regret of things that I did or failed to do. Here the break is absolute. This is also what Spinoza teaches us. Living in the present entirely negates living for the present which is nothing but living for the moment. Living for the moment is mired in the past. This is incompatible with living in the present.

2. Activities Internally Guided

Our activities need to be internally guided and directed. Internal consistency and self-guidance should not be interpreted literally or mechanically. The person must be the final interpreter and judge of his or her life. Personal discretion (at work, with family, etc.) will always be circumscribed by the requirements of others. We must listen to others, and most of all, be considerate of others, but the responsibility for what we do and for what we fail to do will always be ours. In the final analysis, self-direction means the awareness of our responsibilities.

3. Consistency With Our Values

To live in the present means to live in accordance with our values, principles and moral code. To voluntarily place the welfare of the community and family ahead of my own is to enhance my well-being in the long run. To act on the basis of narrow and immediate self-interest is shortsighted and selfish. Such actions appear to serve myself, while in truth they do not. Therefore, they are not based on reason. "We may, under the guidance of reason, seek a greater good in the future in preference to a lesser good in the present, and we may seek a lesser evil in the present in preference to a greater evil in the future" (EIV, 66).

4. Meaningful Work

To live in the present means to derive joy and satisfaction from our work. That does not mean that we can turn our work into some pleasurable and joyful activity at will. It means, that we must seek out all and every oppportunity to make our work meaningful and enjoyable. We have to heighten our continuous involvement and interest in our work, to improve, widen, and enrich our work opportunities and working conditions without violating the objective requirement of the work place. That is the meaning and function of enriching the work content that is open to the individual. Even in the most limited and most prescribed job situations, opportunities for job enrichment abound. Such possibilities need be explored and acted upon, if we are concerned with living in the present.

5. Using Our Time Productively and Creatively

If I feel that my time is being wasted, there is the acccompanying feeling of guilt that prevents me from coming fully alive and from feeling at ease with myself or with others. The right use of my time, the proper balance between work and recreation is an individual matter, it can only be defined by me. But I have to build structure into my daily life. That will prevent me from a tendency toward physical or mental laziness. Inertia, laziness, and a tendency to waste time are strong pulls that act on the person. The conquest of inertia through self discipline is a satisfying inner experience. It gives the individual a renewed sense of self-respect and provides the person with a source of spiritual strength that restores a healthy balance to his or her existence.

6. The Need for Movement and Growth

One of the person's deepest needs is the awareness and the satisfaction of a feeling of personal movement. It includes new learning, increased understanding, or creative activity, every day. A feeling of steady movement and growth lends internal strength to the person. We can face challenge or adversity with calm and detachment. We are not easily thrown off balance. A feeling of personal movement and growth makes our fears, doubts, anxieties, and personal reproaches disappear, as if by magic. We are free to experience fully our real nature. Amazing how our real nature can so often be buried under the burdens of everyday existence, if we don't take the necessary measures to prevent this from happening. Let us consider a hypothetical example: By way of example, we will examine the complexity of human existence, and subject the existentially and phenomenologically exhibited inner conflict to a resolution under the guidance of reason. The example is of a rational approach to life's problems, and an indication of what Spinoza had in mind, when he defined the free person as the one who acts in accordance with reason. "For, insofar as we are intelligent beings, we cannot desire anything save that which is necessary,....wherefore, in so far as we have a right understanding of these things, the endeavour of the better part of ourselves is in harmony with the order of nature as a whole" (EIV, App. 32).

Suppose a person's fundamental nature is optimistic and forward looking, full of joy, vigor, initiative, and faith. Yet these good qualities are not free to assert themselves. So the person must cultivate modes of life that will allow life forces to expand and the spirit to exhilarate. If people do that, they will feel basically satisfied and nothing really can put them down.

We may pose a critical question: How is it that someone with such exceptional qualities can still go through life experiencing mental states just the opposite of his or her potential true self, namely, mental letdowns, dispirited moods, frustrations, and feelings of dissatisfaction or failure? We must fully account for existential dissatisfaction in light of potential exhilaration. The reasons may include the following:

6.1. A Failure To Self- Confront

Supreme effort and pain are required to confront oneself, wholly, radically, and mercilessly, without remorse, and without self-pity. The self-analysis and self-exposure needs to be done in a spirit of total objectivity, to reach the proper conclusions of one's existence.

Subsidiary consequences of the lack of radical self- confrontation include:

6.2. Procrastination of Hard Work and Hard Effort

A tendency to give in to soft living, soft plans for the future, anticipating states of mind which bring pleasurable sensations (musing, nature walks, listening to music). Unfortunately, the longer the person does that, the harder to break such progressively fixed patterns of existence. They become a dominant life style. (Objective conditions must permit the person to do this, namely, he or she must have enough free time at hand.) The individual can thus gradually sink into a state of relative inactivity, interspersed with short outbreaks of frenzied creative work.

6.3. Tendency Toward Extreme Choices (Either/or Criteria)

In viewing situations and work projects in terms of either/ or criteria we expect complete satisfaction or rewards from our work, without accepting the limitations of our nature, the shortcomings of our projects, or the imperfections of life. We expect our life projects to have significance before we embark on them and before we carry them out. This is a flawed approach to our work and therefore bound to failure. Any potentially significant work does not come into being by expectation or wish. It can only come into being by doing. This approach of expecting our work to have significance, *a priori,* is irrational. Worth or significance are first of all relative, and secondly, they are an expression of effort and work performed. To expect significance from our work before we embark on it, would by its nature negate the work and cancel the effort. This is one of the grossest fallacies and a sure way to fail in our intended objectives. It is an example of a lack of a realistic self- assessment and self-appreciation. It may be summed up as a series of self-reinforcing tendencies: Joyful procrastination turning into habitual procrastination coupled with an attitude of self-importance (only significant or great work is worth doing), which leads to a rationalization of plain laziness and the inability for sustained effort. This phenomenon is quite common in the academic profession.

6.4.   Existential Impasse

The inability or willingness to resolve our personal situation in terms of our emotional needs (to share our life in love and sorrow with someone close), while at the same time, we refuse to accept our status as is. We are thus caught in a vicious circle which is difficult to break from. We delay work until we settle down, and we are unable to settle down because of our inability to concentrate and work. The prolonged state of isolation, lack of discipline, lack of concentration, distraction, only worsen the same conditions from which we are trying to break loose, making it harder to change. This requires taking a hold of ourselves.

7. Taking a Hold of Ourselves

Taking a hold of ourselves necessitates the following steps:

1. We must start from where we are, that is, from now, not from yesterday.

2. We must make a radical break with our past adverse patterns of existence and conditioning, such as illusory hopes, postponements, and

delusions. Reality has a way of catching up with us, in a merciless way. Our objective situation suddenly appears in front of us in its most naked form.

3.   A recognition that by living in reality we can still realize our essence regardless of the years gone by. A recognition that with basic outward-looking, life-asserting and faith-embracing attitudes, life can still be exhilarating. To live in reality means to accept our essential self and not to compromise on its essence.

8. The Practice of Self-Discipline

Through the practice of self-discipline and self- understanding, we can neutralize possible adverse external conditions and turn them to our advantage. The most adverse external conditions are those of personal isolation. We experience neither love nor friendship. Yet, we can turn these around through self-understanding. As we get connected with ourselves, with our work, and with others, the condition of isolation will disappear.

To avoid a merely passive existence, we must expand our experiences in all areas of our life. This will bring about the self-assurance that we are in charge of ourselves, and that we are not just being tossed around by events from the outside. We have to come to grips with the basic question of our existence and know what it means to be alive. To live well in the present means to grow mentally, intellectually, emotionally, physically, morally, and in every dimension of life. It means to be self-creative, to express ourselves in our interactions, and to give meaning to our existence. Most of all, it means to give and receive love.

9. The Question of Purpose - Restated

The question of our central purpose is not easy to answer. The question of purpose is an evolving process of self- confrontation and self-searching. We have to know our essence to answer the purpose.

Being true to our essential nature provides us with steadiness, firmness, and balance. Therefore, we need to look at those actions and circumstances of our being that bring us such feelings. We must differentiate between transient and sustained feelings of satisfaction.

Transient feelings come about due to incidental causes. If such transient feelings however, are also related to the individual's essential being, they will tend to be stronger and longer lasting. We might look backwards into our past and consider the times we felt exhilarated as a result of certain actions. We can identify certain behavior patterns and thus learn indirectly about our true nature. We may also find that the objective we have been pursuing for some time has been a false and an unreal one. This may be a sobering realization. It will take us back to a renewed assessment of our basic values and beliefs.

III. PRINCIPLES, VALUES, AND BEHAVIOR

The fundamental aspect of people's values is the degree of clarity and awareness that they possess with respect to their ordering and significance. It presupposes a clearly defined order of priorities. The people that have been able to sort out the different values and recognize their importance to them, are able to make decisions that reflect their values and are therefore less likely to undergo unresolved value conflicts. Individuals assign value to some object or intangible trait because the possession of such valued objects or traits would enhance their existence. Every person lives according to some values. These values are reflected in the choices the person makes. They are called "operative values." The person will not necessarily be conscious of the values that underlie his or her behavior. That is, where the conflict between the values that the person professes to believe (his or her assertive values), and the operative values that underlie his or her behavior, may originate. A sampling of common American values includes the following: Belief in individual drive, achievement, and successs (individual competitiveness), pursuit of materialist goals, viewing life from a short-term perspective, and in general, taking a negative view of human nature. People are usually portrayed in a hierarchical rather than lateral order, placing others above or below instead of on the same footing.

The split between operative and assertive values reveals itself when the individual expresses values that are contrary or inconsistent with the way he or she lives. People with a strong value orientation will normally exhibit a high sense of integrity. That means that they will tend to resolve or minimize any conflict between the way they live and the values they believe in. Strong moral values include a sense of social justice, the need to make a contribution to society through our work, the search for and upholding of truth regardless of personal consequence, high respect for ourselves and for others, considering others on the same level as ourselves, a strong sense of personal integrity and principled behavior, overall strength of character, independence of thought, and the freedom to be oneself. Such strong personal values usually go together with corresponding interpersonal values, such as, human dignity, kinship of human beings, love, caring, understanding, kindness, goodness of heart, tenderness, compassion, gentleness, spontaneity, self confidence, generosity, and a strong sense of personal identity.

1. Possible Sources of Value Conflict

The strength of commitment and the strength of belief are interconnected but not identical traits of the person. Commitment is a matter of character, while belief may be conditioned by other factors. People may profess to similar (moral, political, social, and religious) values, but they will not pursue them with equal strength. Their commitment to their professed values will not be the same. The conflict will reveal itself in situations that call for personal sacrifice. Does strength of character necessitate a readiness of personal sacrifice for our beliefs when the choices are clear? The answer is yes, but situations in life are seldom that clear. Given the inherent tendency toward rationalization, the conflict between belief and conduct will defy easy solutions.

Conflicting pressures upon our behavior may originate from the outside (peer group), or from the inside (conflicted values or goals). It may reflect a lack of clarity about our value priorities or a certain pretense about our character strength. However, a strong sense of self-integrity will eventually lead us to our own truth and will help bring about a resolution of the inner conflict. Integrity means to be true to our feelings, inclinations, dispositions, awareness of strength and weakness of character, without deception and without fear. Integrity precedes commitment. Commitment without integrity is opportunistic. It is a masked commitment. It is not a commitment to anything beyond the individual himself. Integrity by itself will not preclude conflict, but it is essential to the resolution of the conflict.

2. The Resolution of Inner Conflict

The resolution of inner conflict involves a clarification and a decision. We must first bring the conflict into the open, that is, into consciousness. The unconscious conflict will show itself in our indecisive behavior and in an uneasy feeling about ourselves, and about what we are doing. To resolve the conflict, we should not mask or deny our feelings. Only when we accept our feelings can we trace them to their true causes. Such causes can be transient or structural (longer lasting.) The transient causes, (for example, an overreaction to some derogatory remark), once they have been looked into and brought into awareness, will quickly dissipate and disappear.

If we cannot find direct causes for our feelings of discomfort or for our restlessness, then we must look deeper into ourselves to discover their underlying nature. Such structural conflicts stay with us to haunt us for a longer time. Their uncovering requires enhanced understanding and self-knowledge.

Temporary situations may exist which will mask and cover up the deeper, structural conflicts. A person may be carried away along a wave of momentary success. Such success will delay the person's need for self-confrontation and the resolution of the person's structural, deep-seated conflicts.

Any resolution of internal conflict requires, as a first step, to make our values explicit. Most of the time, we carry our beliefs within us, and we do not spell them out even to ourselves. By the sheer act of spelling our values out to ourselves, we will clarify them and perhaps reexamine them. To state and redefine our values is the first step in conflict resolution.

The next step is to examine and reexamine the nature, meaning, implications, and strength of our desire to uphold these values. Both of these steps are fairly simple, but they require utmost self-honesty and patience. They are lengthy processes that can only be shortened in proportion to the individual's determination to find the truth, and to remove obstacles on his or her way to personal growth. They might require a willingness to free ourselves from hitherto cherished beliefs that turned out to be false and which came about purely as a result of past conditioning. They might involve a revision, modification, and or reconfirmation of the person's basic beliefs and values. This is akin to Nietzsche's "transvaluation of all values." The changing of the person's values will enable the person to gain greater clarity and introspection into himself or herself and will engender the process of purification and distillation of the person's beliefs. This will help remove vagueness and self-doubt. The process of value distillation will lead to a renewed commitment to our basic beliefs, whose clarity and purity has been ascertained. This will bring joy to the person.

A reciprocal relationship exists between our ability to be ready to reject all "prior" values and our joy and rededication to the reconfirmed values. The reconfirmed values are truly our own personal values, since we had the choice of rejecting them. They were no longer implanted from the outside.

After the process of distillation, purification, and reconfirmation of our values, we should decide about their respective priorities. How do the various values relate to each other, and what is their importance on a hierarchical value scale? Which value is of such basic importance that it cannot be violated? That value (or set of values) becomes a principle.

A principle is a value that we will not normally violate. A principle that we will not violate under any conditions is the highest principle. The recognition of principled behavior means that there exists some principle of the highest order for which we would be ready to sacrifice our life in order to uphold it. For example, I reconfirm my respect for my father and mother, and I am confident in my commitment to protect them in the face of death. The self-confidence that emanates from such inner resolution and knowledge that I would rather die than let anyone dishonor my parents, gives me inner strength and it lends firmness and guidance to my actions. Such principled commitment holds for any value that we are willing to uphold and suffer for its upholding. For Spinoza, truth was such a highest principle.

Other values may rise to the order of principles, but they may not be as absolute as the highest principle. A flexibility of behavior is required to live a principled life. The process of personal value examination ("a transvaluation of all values") may reveal values that the person has outgrown or discarded. For example, as we become more independent and free, conformity as a value will gradually lose its appeal to us. Similarly, we will experience less of a need for praise or for outside recognition as our self-confidence increases and as we get stronger.

After we have clarified our values and reassessed their importance to us, we will be able to correct our behavior in line with our renewed understanding of ourselves. The compatibility of behavior with principled beliefs and values implies not only the examination of what we do, but also of what we fail to do. We can easily correct what we do, but much more difficult is to deal with what we fail to do. What we fail to do lacks the necessary concreteness and may not be readily understood. The problem is nevertheless real. The failure to do something that we ought to do, or the failure to do it well enough, may be the cause of a nagging feeling of inadequacy. This will necessitate making our moral standards, ideals, and aspirations, explicit. The latter needs to be done to get a more concrete grasp of these inner voices and feelings of self-censure. We have to explore all potential opportunities that will deepen our mind and strengthen our body. The process of self-actualization and personal growth is never ending.

Notes

1. Foistad, Guttorm, *Reality or Perfection,* in Hessing, S. ed. *Speculum Spinozanum; A Kaleidoscopic Homage,* 1677-1977, London, pp.165-169.
2. Gilles Deleuze, *Expressionism in Philosophy: Spinoza,* New York: Zone Books, 1990, p.192.
3. Benedict De Spinoza, *Short Treatise on God, Man and His Well Being,* Opera, ed. Carl Gebhardt, Heidelberg: Winter, 1924, vol.1, p.87.
4. Immanuel Kant, *Prolegomena to Any Future Metaphysics,* transl. by Lewis White Beck, New York: Macmillan Publishing Company, 1989, p.92.
5. Jean Paul Sartre, *Being and Nothingness,* New York: Washington Square Press, 1966, p.623.
6. J. Van Vloten, Spinoza: An Oration, in *Spinoza; Four Essays,* William Knight, ed. Edinburgh: Williams and Norgate 1882, p.141.

7.   R. Travers Herford, *The Ethics of the Talmud; Sayings of the Fathers*, New York: Schocken Books, 1962, p.34.

8.   F. W. J. von Schelling *Of Human Freedom*. Chicago: Open Court Publishing, Co. 1936. pp.45-46.

9.   Rabbi Chanina Ben Dosa used to say: "He whose deeds exceed his wisdom, his wisdom endures, but he whose wisdom exceeds his deeds, his wisdom does not endure." *Mishnayoth, Tractate Avoth, Ethics of the Fathers*, ed. by Philip Blackman, F.C.S., New York: Judaica Press, 1964, p.60.

CHAPTER 9
LOVE AND FRIENDSHIP: THE OVERCOMING OF SELF-ALIENATION

1.Self- Alienation

We have referred to alienation as a pervasive phenomenon of our culture and society. People fail to acknowledge the common humanity in each other. This is the primary cause of social misery and spiritual impoverishment characteristic of a consumer oriented society. It even intrudes into the family. The increased breakdown of families cannot be separated from the general cultural alienation prevailing in the society at large.

To counteract alienation I have to begin with myself. To overcome alienation means to remove the barrier that exists between me and others (at work, at home, on the block,). This is only posssible when I realize that the barrier that separates me from the other is to be found in the first instance within me and not within the other. Alienation is first and foremost self- alienation. Only to the extent that I get to know myself better and accept myself can I try to remove that barrier that separates me from others. The more I accept myself, and the more I can be myself in whatever I do, the less alienated will I be from other people. "Self approval is in reality the highest object for which we can hope" (EIV, 42, Note).

To be secure within myself means to be less concerned about how others view me. I need not unduly worry about my image and about my appearance to others. When I am insecure, I am more concerned with protecting my turf, my reputation, and my ego. I may become arrogant. I protect myself by putting the other down. Or, I become judgmental. I build fences around myself, either through arrogance, or by being overly self-conscious and trying to protect myself from the intrusion of the other. The consequence of this is that my behavior becomes cramped, unfree, unspontaneous, and artificial. I am not relating to the other from the inner core of my being. I cannot therefore get connected to the other. The true cause of this is, that I am not really connected myself with the inner core of my being, since I am more concerned with appearance rather than with essence. Now, if the other is just as alienated from himself as I am from myself, then human interactions become empty of real content. Human relations become superficial and mechanical.

To overcome my own alienation means to enhance my freedom to be myself, or simply, the freedom to be. It means to bring my existence in line with my essence. I can become more free only to the extent that I am the true cause of my actions, that is , when my activity is self-directed and my powers to act are thereby enhanced. I will get away from my preoccupation with myself or with my image.

The best way to overcome feelings of alienation is by developing and deepening our areas of interest, whether in our work or ouside it. We must look for intrinsic rewards from our work or from our activities. We get connected thereby to the outside as well as to the inside of ourselves.

To the extent that we cultivate and deepen our intrinsic interest in our activities we will connect with others from a genuine source of our being. When I develop a deep interest in any area of knowledge, my self-esteem is enhanced. Thus Spinoza advises his friend: "I should like to ask you, nay I do beg and entreat you, by our friedship, to apply yourself to some serious work with real study, and to devote the chief part of your life to the cultivation of your understanding and your soul" (Letter 41.A. to I. Bresser). This self-esteem will solidify and grow with our experiences in life. Our self-esteem will depend less and less on the acquisition of material things. It will get more and more elevated to a higher, spiritual plane. My creativity is enhanced thereby, because genuine interest is the application of my uniqueness to some segment of the outside world. This shift in focus away from myself toward the outside of me connects me in a deeper sense with my surroundings. As my preoccupation with myself diminishes, my awareness of the other is heightened. My sensitivity is increased. My senses become sharper. I see more and penetrate deeper than before. Because I am not conscious of my external self, I can be more free to be my real self. I can relate to others on the basis of respect and dignity.

The above is largely the application of Martin Buber's I -Thou principle to interpersonal relations.[1] It involves the recognition of a shared humanity in each of us. This feeling of shared humanity guides my interactions with others, from the most casual to the most intimate. The philosophy of the I and Thou is the philosophy of the sphere of the "in between" where true and genuine dialogue takes place. The spoken or unspoken word is its living context. In genuine encounter, I confirm you in your being as I am confirmed by you in my being. The sphere of the interhuman, as distinct from the social, is the sphere where people are present to each other. I am present with my whole undivided being for you, in the here and now. Being present reveals my inner self (my uniqueness) to me as well as to you. My whole being is fully engaged in meeting you. I relate to you as the unique you that you are. In this I affirm you as I affirm myself. In meeting you I am becoming more alive. Aliveness is concrete, and present in the encounter between me and you. The encounter points to the existential truth of you and me.

Suppose a stranger asks for direction. I immediately open up and turn my attention to him. Non-verbally, I express respect and understanding. This will normally bring a reciprocal reaction from the other person towards me. Alienation being a social phenomenon, I cannot hope to entirely overcome it. The least I can do is to be aware of it and work on it. To be completely free of self-alienation is the same as to achieve total freedom. I can go toward it, but I can hardly get there.

Suppose, I meet a friend. My face lights up. It expresses joy. We enjoy being together. We listen to each other with understanding. We give support and encouragement, when needed. The relaxed conversation, the sincerity of our interest and care for each other invigorates our mutual sense of well- being and strengthens our spirit. The encounter with my friend has reinforced me as a person. It has made me stronger. I can now face the day's problem's or frustrations with greater ease and self-confidence.

When two people in love meet, they might blush a little. They might experience a slight tremor of anxiety. This is so, because they might not yet feel sufficiently secure in the relationship. When love enters our person, a sense of dependency comes along. There is some fear of inadequacy or doubt of being fully accepted. In this fear, I tend to exaggerate my weakness. Will my beloved accept me the way I am and help me grow as the person that I am? I cannot know this fully. Hence, the slight tremor of agitation. I long for perfection in love. But I am not perfect. Therefore I become anxious. I tend to deny or hide my weakness from myself. By doing that, I am forcing the other to deny what he or she sees in me. This undermines trust. The integrity of the relationship is at stake. Self-denial and self-deception need to be removed to allow the relationship to unfold and grow. Love is not possible without the foundation of trust.

When two people in love are sufficiently secure within themselves to face themselves honestly and without fear, they will also be able to accept each other the way they are, with their respective flaws and shortcomings. The sense of trust that builds up between them will help each other overcome their respective developmental blocks. This turns perceived weakness into strength. The bond between lovers becomes steeled in life's ordeals and trials. When tested by misfortune or tragedy, their love for each other becomes stronger and purer. Here, the I-Thou principle reaches its highest expression.

Spinoza does not discuss the nature of human intimacy at any length. His entire *Ethics* however, provides ample ground for a philosophical understanding of the nature of love and friendship. For Spinoza, the highest love that we can achieve is the intellectual love of God. But this in no way minimizes the importance of love and intimacy in human relationships. In what follows, I discuss the nature of love and friendship based on Spinoza's spirit rather than the letter. I develop my approach to human intimacy from the basic tenets of Spinoza's philosophy of life. The discussion is from an existential perspective.

2. The Nature of Love

We may begin our discussion with the fundamental question: what is the nature of love?

That mysterious aspect of a relationship which is called love cannot be put into words. Love starts as a reflection of some aspect of the person that is strongly appealing to the other. All other aspects (qualities) of the person may for the time being be suppressed. If the attraction is based primarily on appearance or on what is shown on the surface, it may result in infatuation rather than love. If objective conditions for the evolution of a relationship exist, that is, if the two people are also compatible in other ways, love may grow.

Intangible values, such as, spiritual, aesthetic, moral, and emotional belong to the realm of the non-material dimensions of life. Their satisfaction enhances the quality and richness of life. Unlike material goods, they can not be produced or exchanged at will. Their use and satisfaction depends entirely on human interaction. Their strength grows with their use, contrary to material goods which are destroyed with use.

Thus, our capacity for giving and receiving love grows with practice. The more we give, the more we receive and the more are we able to give and receive love. On the other hand, if we give love without ever receiving love in return, the source of our love will dry up.

Non-material values cannot be divided into smaller parts or measured on a quantitative scale. Love in its multitude of forms (affection, acceptance, forgiveness,) is so basic to human well-being, that we cannot survive as a wholesome person without it. While love can be expressed and manifested in infinite ways and in many degrees of intensity, we cannot produce it through human labor or at will.

Unfortunately, people lose their capacity for love as they become more alienated from others. A lack of love leads to a progressive and gradual disintegration of the entire person. The individual loses his or her human qualities. He or she may continue to exist and function, but they will do so in an inhuman, machine-like, or mechanical manner. The lack of love takes away the person's human essence. The person loses his or her human face. Without food, we lose our physical existence. Without love, we lose our being.

Love is distinctly a human quality. Nature provides for the necessary care and affection needed to raise animals. But this animal love is based on instinct. It is only present to guarantee the continuity of the species. It is nature's way to safeguard the survival of the species. All instincts are ultimately survival instincts.

Human love is intimately bound up with human life. Love is needed not for mere physical survival, but to survive as a human being. Love is the culmination and the universal expresssion of all that is good in us, of the best feelings that we have toward each other. All these feelings come from the same source, our heart.

Other intangible values, such as kindness, goodness of heart, and compassion are individual expressions towards people in general. Love is pointed and directed towards a concrete person or persons. It is a concentrated expression of the generalized value (kindness, tenderness, goodness, compassion,) that is focused on a particular person. We may assume, that an individual who lacks the generalized human values (toward humanity) does not possess the source whence love originates.

Let us not confuse real or existential love with the ideal of love. Idealized love is not real because it does not exist and because it cannot be attained. Its appearance may only take the form of infatuation which is not the same as love. Real love contains elements of frustration, friction, even sadness, all of which are parts of the harsh realities of daily life. Our love necesarily reflects the imperfections inherent in being human. This is not the case with Plato's view of love. For Plato, love is primarily the love of beauty. Love is made contingent on the beautiful. It is a highly idealized form of love. It does not want to recognize the ugliness and the seemy side of life. In Plato's *Symposium*, Diotima says: "One should possess beauty forever." Human tenderness and affection do not play a significant part in Plato's notion of love. Beauty is the essence of love, but it is closely connected with the idea of the good, which is its embodiment. Love as beauty bridges the world of things with the world of ideas. It serves as a bridge between the particular and the universal. The highest beauty is confined to the world of Forms and the world of Ideas.

The insistence on ideal rather than on real love leads to a distortion of reality, and therefore precludes the possibility of its realization. The need for genuine warmth and real intimacy is strictly a human attribute. Passive love (the need to be loved) is conditioned by active loving (the need to give love). The mutuality of feelings underlie the need for love. Unfortunately, a genuine mutuality of feelings is not as common as is the need for it. Everybody wants to be loved, but many fail to practice the art of giving love. To be able to give love is an art that needs to be developed through the actual practice of it.[2] To want to be loved without developing our capacity to love and without simultaneously giving love, is for the most part, an idle pursuit.

A genuine relationship is possible even if partial rather than total. For as long as we have genuine feelings without pretense for each other, the need for love can be partially satisfied. Exclusive, romantic love is more than that. It implies a mutuality of endeavors and an infinitude of mutual trust that absorbs each partner as a whole person while simultaneously upholding the individuality of each.

Love gives reality to individual dreams by daring them. Reality and dreams merge and become indistinguishable from each other. We walk on the ground and it feels like walking on a cloud. Reality gets a dream-like quality and distant dreams acquire a real-like appearance. Subconscious dreams present themselves with concrete forcefulness. Love is a conspiracy of two people to make their dreams come true. The fusion of the lovers' futures gives strength to the individuality of each. As time passes, as the future turns into the present and the present recedes into the past, people in love grow in inner strength and beauty. They become fountains that overflow with wisdom, understanding, and compassion. Their individual lives gradually transcend their physical selves, and they become sources of strength and joy to themselves and to all those around them. Their life is transformed from the exclusiveness of the two into the joy of being and giving to others. They share themselves, their work, their knowledge and experience with the rest of humanity. This brings us to friendship.

3. Friendship

Friendship between people contains an objective element (the things that the individuals have in common and share with each other), as well as a subjective element which is intangible. This intangible element is simply the enjoyment derived from being together. It has all the ingredients of love except for the physical and sexual attraction that underlies romantic love between two people. This is the essence of ideal friendship.

Real friendship will necessarily deviate from the ideal in several ways. However, for friendship to exist in real-life situations, both the objective and the subjective elements of the relationship must be present. This sharing and the enjoying of each other's presence must be there in actual friendship though not necessarilly to the fullest degree required by the ideal.

Perhaps the closest model of the fusion of friendship with love is to be found in the *"Confessions"* by St. Augustine. It describes the unique relationship of St. Augustine with his mother Monica. Their relationship rests on the purity and strength of their extraordinary characters. The beauty of their relationship is almost unsurpassed in the whole of world literature. The intimacy betwen mother and son, the reaching out to each other from the depth of their hearts, the total lack of false feelings or cheap sentimentality, as well as the unshaken bond and love between them can be vividly seen whenever they are together. The scene at Ostia on the Tiber, at Monica's approaching death, is beautiful beyond description.[3] Monica faces death realistically, without any regrets or artificial desires. Her greatest wish in this world (that her son become a true believer) has been fulfilled, and now she is ready to depart from the world in the joy of knowing God. Her faith in God has never been stronger. The beauty and the strength of their love and friendship can be easily glimpsed from the following passage: "We were alone, conversing together most tenderly, forgetting those things that are behind, and stretching forth to those that are before."[4]

One of the best treatments of friendship is given by Aristotle, in the *Nicomachean Ethics.*[5] Aristotle differentiates between higher and lower forms of friendship. Perfect friendship exists between people who share similar interests (activities) and are alike in virtue. Such friendship is without any qualification or special reason. Lower forms of friendship are motivated by the expectation of utility or pleasure. These kinds of friendship do not endure. True friends reflect each other's virtues and wish well for each other from their natures. They contemplate each other's happiness, activities. Aristotle, defines happiness as the final end, the highest and the most sufficient good. "Happiness is....the end of action."[6] It is activity in accordance with the highest excellence and virtue. True friends are more interested in giving than getting, in loving than being loved. For "love is like activity, being loved like passivity".[7] The love of a friend is like the love of oneself. We love ourselves for our sake, for being ourselves and for the rational part in us. To love ourselves and others, is to esteem the *nous* in ourselves and in others. *Nous* is distinct from reason because it is pure rationality (intelligence) without any calculative quality. It is the most divine element in us. We love our friends for the same reasons and in the same way as we love ourselves. With friends, we exist and act better and our life is most fulfilled. We exist by "living and acting," and people choose to exist and love existence.[8] People who are most attuned to life (activity) are the happiest, their life is good and pleasant. Friendships among virtuous men or women is most sublime, since each desires for him or herself what he or she desires for the other. We grow in goodness through friendship, and we are more able to think and act with friends than without them.[9] True friends permit and uphold the identity of each other. Such friendship is the highest expression of the freedom of each.

Socrates accepts the Aristotelian view of true friendship as that between people who are alike in virtue. Friends must know each other, open up to each other, and be like each other in virtue. For Plato, however, the "good" is the end of friendship.[10] The implication is that people become friends for the sake of some gain. Socrates qualifies this, by telling Lysis that since childhood he wanted to have a true (good) friend more "than all the gold of Darius." Socrates concludes the dialogue in *Lysis* by suggesting that Lysis and Menexenus are true friends because they are akin to each other. Friends get to be like each other and identify with each other. This is also seen in St. Augustine, when he describes his lost friend: "for we have become one soul residing in two bodies."[11]

Becoming like each other in friendship is not the same as becoming indistinct from each other. Quite to the contrary, individuality and distinctness are developed within friendship. True friends love each other but they do not possess each other. For Socrates, the need for friendship and for genuine conversation was the primary motif of his life.

For Aristotle, lower forms of friendship are seen when the sharing is restricted to specific activities with a view to their utility. Even here for any friendship to exist, the involvement of the two people in their limited ways must encompass each one as a whole person. For the subjective aspect of the relationship provides the background for the mutual appreciation and enjoyment of each other. If the subjective element is missing and the sharing of interest is limited, then the two people perform a simple service or function for each other. Or they may be using each other for their own convenience.

4. The Existential Dimension of Friendship

Exaggerated self-absorption, self-preoccupation and self-centeredness are impediments to friendship. Self-centered individuals are unable to form true friendships. Self-centered people are handicapped in their ability to extend themselves fully to others. They are selfish and will not inconvenience themselves for others. True friendship is based primarily on giving and only secondarily on getting. People who are insensitive to the needs of others, and who are calculative in their relationships, are unable to give much comfort and moral support to others.

Spinoza does not discuss at length the existential dimension of friendship. He does not describe the trials and travails of human bonds and relationships. He neverthless points to its general direction. He greatly valued the true bonds of friendship, both for their spiritual as well as practical importance. The following passages attest to that:

When "two individuals of entirely the same nature are united, they form a combination twice as powerful as either of them singly. Therefore, to man there is nothing more useful than man...."(EIV, 18, Note).

"the free man only desires to join other men to him in friendship."

"only free men are thoroughly useful one to another, and associated among themselves by the closest necessity of friendship..." (EIV, 61. Schol.).

"So far as in me lies, I value, above all other things out of my control, the joining hands of friendship with men who are sincere lovers of truth" (Letter 32 to Blyenbergh).

"between friends all things, and especially things spiritual ought to be in common" (Letter 2 to Oldenburg).

Spinoza considered friendship of vital importance for the good life. Friendship, like everything else in life, is a matter of degree. In the remaining part of this chapter, I focus on the existential dimension of friendship in real-life situations, and its evolution or its failure to evolve, between any two people.

Several components enter into the making of friendship, including trust, mutual acceptance, shared interests, and values.   If we, for convenience sake, would range these components on a scale of 1 to 10, we may find that two individuals will normally be situated at different ranges on the comparative attribute scale. This helps us evaluate the scope of an existing friendship between people. We may even range the attributes of the composite friendship relation and devise a scale for each. People will normally find themselves at different locations on the corresponding attribute scales. Over time, as friendship develops or fails to develop, the locations on the attribute scales will change. A movement toward the upper range indicates growth, while a movement toward the lower range of the scale indicates regression or decline.

Friendship, like love rests on mutuality. One sided relationships that inhere in individual advantage are often disguised as friendship. Even in genuine friendships, we will not find perfect reciprocity. One person may be more trusting, more giving, more accepting, more considerate. As long as the divergence between the two people on the composite friendship scale is not too great, their friendship will continue, and grow.

Mutuality of interest and shared values are the foundation of friendship. Yet not every encounter between two people who share similar values and interests will lead to an enduring relationship between them. Objective conditions, such as, proximity in age, status, place, and personal circumstance must also be present for friendship to develop.

Friendship between two people may be genuine and real, but due to objective crcumstances, it may also be partial and incomplete. For example, two people may always enjoy each other's company, feel free in each other's presence, are stimulated by each other, and wish each other well. They are well matched in terms of mutuality of interest and compatibilty of intellect. Yet there may be a drawback to this relationship in terms of physical distance or another impediment that inhibits the possibility of regular encounter. On the other hand, a relationship may be genuine, and yet some essential element may be missing. There may be insufficient excitement and stimulation, or the two people may not fully accept each other. While they genuinely share some special interests (say, story telling), they are unable to develop a full friendship, due to a lack of other necessary attributes between them.

5. The Quality of the Relationship

In general, we may say that the quality of friendship is based on the following:

1. Mutual attraction and interest in each other, and 2. mutuality and reciprocity of trust. Trust enables the two people to open up to each other and to feel secure with each other. We are inclined to become friends with people who are similar to us in character. Each of us exhibits character traits that we may like or dislike in ourselves or in another. A useful exercise would be to list those character traits that we admire and those that we dislike. This will help us gain clarity about ourselves and others. It will also help in our effort to change the less desirable characteristic behavior traits. In this effort to achieve firmness of mind and strength of character, Spinoza serves as a beacon of light, a great teacher, and a role

model for us to learn from. I enumerate those personality traits that would appeal to Spinoza and to me.

The most important human quality is strength of character and firmness of mind. This will include: self-acceptance, thoughtfulnes, genuineness of behavior, personal integrity and loyalty, sense of commitment, physical and moral courage, independence of mind and thought, personal modesty, simplicity, and dignity. In addition to these, we would greatly value a person's superior intellect and intelligence, his or her acute sensitivity, a subtleness of taste and expression, a good sense of humor, and an existential innocence and childlikeness. These traits would appeal to Spinoza. For Spinoza, our strength and freedom lies in the courage and nobility of character (IV, 63, Note). And, "he that is strong hates no man, is angry with no man, envies no man, is indignant with no man, despises no man, and least of all things is proud" (EIV, 63, Note). Some less desirable character traits would appeal least to Spinoza. Those would probably include: greed, aggressiveness, boastfulness, pretense, compulsiveness, manipulative or calculative behavior, and selfishness as distinct from self interest. Positive character traits are the foundation for a lasting friendship between people.

However, any relationship between people involves effective communication as its base, which proceeds on verbal and non-verbal levels. Non-verbal communication requires sensitivity to cues emanating from others and the ability to interpret these correctly. People who are in tune with each other are able to read each other correctly. This greatly facilitates mutual understanding and the enjoyment of one another. The spoken words also need to be correctly understood and interpreted. The non-verbal clues help us to receive and correctly interpret the verbal messages. This requires a willingness to listen along with the practice of the art of good listening.

Bonds of friendship between two people may grow or diminish with time. When people identify their well-being in terms of each other's welfare, the bonds of their friendship will get stronger. "A person who contributes to other peoples' security, contributes to his own."[12] People in such relationships derive gratification primarily from giving rather than from receiving. They think of the other person from the vantage point of the other rather than from their viewpoint. "In human relations we must constantly be alert to the emotions, sentiments, attitudes, perceptions and ideas of others."[13] Thus, we need to pay attention to facial expressions, bodily postures, gestures, vocal intonations, and eye contact of the other.

When the two individuals become routinely more self centered, their relationship is bound to deteriorate. A decline in effective communication, understanding, and sensitivity result. A deterioration in the quality of listening to each other takes place. Eventually they become more self-preoccupied, and their interest in each other declines. Unless corrective action is taken, a breakdown of the relationship is unavoidable. But beware of absolutes. In any ongoing relationship there are recurrent lapses that lead to misunderstanding, faulty communication, lack of sensitivity, and self-preoccupation. The real test of the quality of a relationship, whether in friendship or in love, is how the two people deal with the problems they encounter. There will always be hurdles in any relationship because the road to closeness is a thorny one. There will always be bumps along the road that have to be smoothed out and overcome. How any two people in a relationship meet and deal with those bumps, is a true test of the strength of their friendship.

Mutual esteem or implicit admiration draws people together. "Approval is love towards one who has done good to another" (EIV, 41, Sch.). As a relationship evolves, people will share more of themselves with each other. Trust is gradually built up. As trust is established, each person feels more at ease and secure within the relationship. Real intimacy between them grows, and the quality of the relationship is thus enhanced.

The quality of any relationship will directly depend on the degree of security and intimacy that each of the individuals feels within it. Real friends never judge or reject the other person as a whole. They will judge or criticize aspects of the other's behavior, but will do this to help, not to reject the other.

The nature of closeness or intimacy is feeling. It is the subjective and spontaneous quality of a relationship. Feeling imbues the relationship with radiant life. This objectively unexplainable quality is unique to the relationship. In this sense, each relationship is unique.

A purely formal or business-like connection between two people may be based on mutual esteem, but it may be lacking in warmth. The relationship will be secure but not close. On the other hand, a relationship between friends may be close, but to the extent that one or the other feels insecure within it (not totally accepted by the other), the relationship will be qualitatively poor. One person will be more dependent or less free than the other.

There is a thin line between security and closeness within a relationship. Real intimacy is not possible without real security. Intimacy involves self disclosure and the satisfaction of emotional need. It involves the freedom to be ourselves in the relationship with the other. This is conditioned by trust. And trust is the basis for security. Superficially, people can be intimate with each other and yet feel insecure, either because of some personal character trait, or because of a feeling of not being fully accepted by the other. Insecurity within a relationship may also result from an imbalance in the dependency needs of the two individuals.

Security is based on acceptance conditioned by the mutuality of respect. To respect another person means: to take the other person seriously; to listen to the other person attentively; not to be condescending to the other person explicitly or implicitly; not to belittle the other person; not to use the other person for one-sided advantage; and, not to exploit the other person's weakness.

Respect is based on shared humanity. It is not conditioned by accomplishment or position. People who are exploitive, manipulative, or who use others for their own ends are not worthy of respect. The respect for human dignity is *a sine qua non* of being respectable.

When a relationship is close but insecure, it will be unstable. Friction, conflict, tension, unresolved difficulties, lack of understanding, and a lack of sensitivity will result. This will not normally be the case when a relationship is fairly secure though not close. When feelings are not invested in a relationship, the fear of rejection is greatly diminished and the security of the person is not threatened thereby.

When the relationship between two people becomes close, security within the relationship becomes most important. Security within a relationship determines the quality of the relationship. The quality of a relationship is directly proportionate to the degree of security each of the individuals feels within it. The lack of necessary synchronization or of one-to-one correspondence between positions on the closeness and security scales open up a variety of possible outcomes. Human relationships are highly complex and subject to many different expressions. The security scale may be viewed as the objective aspect of the relationship, the mutuality of respect and recognition. The closeness scale may be taken to indicate the subjective aspect of the relationship, love and feeling. Love and respect are the most important indicators of the true nature of a relationship.

The essence of closeness (feeling, love) is not restricted to elation or happiness. Feelings of sadness are just as part of closeness as happiness. Objective conditions may cause loss, misunderstanding, or friction. A crisis in the relationship may follow. However, if the relationship is qualitatively strong, the closeness of the two people will increase and happiness will follow adversity. The bonds between two people in love or in friendship will have strengthened in the face of adversity and crisis. On the other hand, when there is insufficient mutual acceptance, trust, and security between the two people, one or the other person will not be able to overcome adversity. Nor will they be able to support each other in times of crisis or loss. The relationship is then likely to suffer and deteriorate under the influence of adverse external conditions.

When the quality of the relationship is not secure, the individuals may engage in a silent (unexpressed) power struggle to safeguard a secure or dominant position *vis a vis* each other. This will bring some element of competition or manipulation into the relationship. One or the other may aspire to be always right, or smart. He or she may develop a dependency upon the other person's reinforcement of his or her exaggerated ego needs. This may result in an unhealthy pattern of relating that assumes a dynamic of its own, independent of the conscious or subconscious desires of each. The two people gradually lose control over the essence and movement of their relationship. Eventually, if this loss of conscious control and of the awareness of an ongoing power struggle is allowed to continue the relationship will deteriorate and perhaps end.

6. The Ending of a Relationship

The ending of a relationship is not necesarily an aspect of physical separation, such as in divorce. A relationship may end even when the two people continue to live together but lose the qualitative attributes of emotional closeness and strength between them. They cease to communicate with each other from the center of their inner selves. To the extent that they talk to each other, their talk is neutral and uninvolved. Or, it may be purely functional. The relationship becomes empty. The death of a relationship is like the death of the body. "I consider that a body undergoes death, when the proportion of motion and rest obtained mutually among its several parts is changed" (EIV, 39, Note).

A body does not die when it becomes a corpse, but when its nature has been entirely transformed. "It sometimes happens that a man undergoes such changes, that I should hardly call him the same" (EIV, 39, Note). We can say the same about a relationship. The relationship is dead when it changes its nature to the extent that we can hardly call it the same.

Ideally, there should not be an attempt to manipulate a relationship for the sake of a desired objective or outcome. However, when readiness for a relationship on the part of one or both of the parties exists, manipulation may not be noticed, or if it is done in the desired direction, it may be welcomed as a sign of love or desire. To the extent that manipulation takes place, there is a corresponding lack of real feeling. Such a lack of real feelings that are not commensurable with expressed feelings may occasionally reveal itself in the omission of some detail, which is characteristic of people in love. It may reveal itself in thoughtlessness or a lack of consideration in a small matter that is of importance to the other party.

To the extent that the will to love, or the will to stay in a relationship, is stronger than the feeling of love, the relationship is bound to be self-centered. Love in such a relationship will be selfish and not other-directed. This leads to a contradiction, since true love, while based on self-love, is always and by necessity the love we feel for the other. This lack of real love will lead to thoughtlesness. On the other hand, thoughtlessness will necesarily reinforce the decline of love. Thoughtlesness is destructive of real love.

Insecurity that results from an imbalance of commitment between the parties will be worsened by a person's lack of self- confidence. A person who lacks a healthy self-respect or one that suffers from feelings of inferiority will exhibit the same in a relationship with another person. This will negatively affect the evolution of the relationship. Inferiority will reinforce emotional insecurity and *vice versa*. The parties involved may fail to grasp clearly or consciously the nature of their insecurity. Most often they will suppress it or deny it. They might get caught in a vicious circle from which they are unable to escape. Occasional down feelings may be interpreted as rejection. This is especially detrimental to the relationship, since the slightly depressed party is in need of consolation, encouragement, emotional support, and good words from the other person. Instead, he or she gets reciprocal gloom brought about by the supposed rejection, which has been internalized by the insecure party.

In general, insecurity leads to anxiety which leads to a loss of spontaneity, which in turn means that the person is not free to be or to give of himself or of herself freely and fully. Anxiety and a loss of freedom will also result if the two people expect different things from the relationship, or if they differ in their readiness to commit themselves to it.

To feel at ease with another person means not to be self- conscious. To be thoughtful of another person means to consider the other person's needs ahead of our own. Thoughtfulness adds beauty and luster to any relationship between two people. The more things the two people have in common, the easier it will be for the relationship to unfold. If they are to stimulate and excite each other, the two individuals should be of a comparable level of intelligence, and share common interests and values. If the gap is too wide, or if it cannot be bridged, then the challenge and the excitement of the relationship will diminish along with the intrigue, enjoyment, and mystery which is called love.

Notes

1. Martin Buber, *I - Thou*. New york: Scribner, 1970.
2. This is well developed in: Erich Fromm, *The Art of Loving*. New York, Evanston: Harper & Row Publishers, 1956.
3. St. Augustine, *Confessions*. "The Vision at Ostia," Book 9, Chap. 10.
4. Ibid. p. 221.
5. Aristotle, *Nicomachean Ethics*, Books VIII and IX.
6. Ibid. 1098 b 20-25.
7. Ibid. 1168 a18.
8. Ibid. 1168 a 5-8.
9. Ibid. 1155a 15-18.
10. See Plato's dialogue *Lysis*.
11. St. Augustine, *Confessions*, Book 4, Chapter 6.
12. F.K. Berrien, *Comments and Cases on Human Relations*. New York: Harpers & Brothers, p. 236.
13. Ibid. p.37.

CHAPTER 10
AUTHENTIC EXISTENCE

1. The Scope of Human Freedom

Our objective in this work was to consider Spinoza's *Ethics* in the context of human existence, as an actually lived life. Life is never without problems, and to live under the guidance of reason becomes the question of how to apply reason to life's problems. Life's problems include conflict, tension, frustration, desires, and hopes. We have concentrated on the existential dimension of Spinoza's *Ethics*. In this chapter we want to take up the question of what to live authentically means, and specifically, the question of the transition from inauthentic to authentic existence.

As part of nature, we are bound to causal necessity. Spinoza's denial of the freedom of the will means that there cannot be a will without a cause, in the sense of Descartes' uncaused will. An uncaused will turns the notion of the will into the same abstraction as that of the mind. Instead, for Spinoza, we have only volitions, desires, perceptions, imaginations, or in other words, ideas. These are subject to the general system of causes in nature. Efficient causation underlies all our actions (and existence). Our behavior is determined by conscious and unconscious desires and motivations. Both the conscious and the unconscious desires operate as efficient causes that affect and determine our actions. The inclusion of our conscious desires as efficient causes means that we have freedom of choice with respect to our actions. This freedom is qualified by the totality of the situation that we find ourselves in. Such freedom is essentially conditioned by the extent that we have adequate or inadequate ideas about ourselves and our situation. To the extent that our conscious desires reflect inadequate ideas, we may choose courses of actions based on one or another set of such ideas. This does not represent real freedom, since our actions and existence is based on the lack of true knowledge of ourselves (inadequate ideas). If on the other hand, we acquire adequate ideas that motivate our actions, such actions will both be necessary and free. We are faced here with two existential problems: one is the acquisition of adequate ideas about ourselves, namely, self-knowledge. The other is the conscious choice and need to act on it. Both of these conditions are necessary for the enhancement of our freedom. We cannot assume that they operate automatically, without our conscious desire to bring them about. The desire to move from inadequate to adequate ideas, from self-ignorance to self-knowledge, as well as the desire to act on true self-knowledge, must both be present if we endeavor to enhance the scope of our freedom.

2. Human Freedom Within the Context of Human Essence: Self- Preservation and Self-Elevation

The law of self-preservation and self-elevation determines the meaning of human freedom. When we have adequate ideas about ourselves and act on them, our actions will necessarily conform to the divine law of our essence, they will necessarily be consistent with our endeavor to self-preserve and self-elevate. Therein lies our true freedom. Our true freedom cannot be exercised against ourselves. The divine essence of self-preservation includes self-elevation. To the extent that we act on ignorance and inadequate ideas about ourselves and the situation in which we find ourselves (our reality), our freedom of choice between alternative means and competing ends is there, but it is a false kind of freedom. Such freedom is illusory and unreal. Only to the extent that we act on adequate ideas and true knowing, will our actions truly be free. In this case, our true freedom (to act) is determined by the truth of the ideas that underlie our actions. To the extent that our actions are based on true ideas, they are both necessary and free. They are necessary because not to do so would mean to act on inadeqate rather than adequate self-knowledge. And they are free because we freely choose to act within the necessity of what is best for us, namely, for the sake of self-preservation and self-elevation. True freedom does not allow us to act contrary to our divine essence. Freedom and necessity are not contraries, they are both true.

We are responsible for our choices. These choices pertain to our fundamental decision to acquire adequate ideas about ourselves, to gain self knowledge, and to act on it. Reason (knowledge) alone is insufficient for right action. Right action requires that an affect (desire) be attached to this knowledge. We may have true knowledge of what is good for us, yet fail to have the corresponding desire for it, for example, smoking or overeating. Thus we will not act on it. This is so, because "Desire arising from the knowledge of good and bad can be quenched or checked by many of the other desires arising from their emotions whereby we are assailed" (EIV, 15). Action attached to true knowledge will only follow when an affect (desire) is present that is stronger than that of any competing desire. Here the notion of responsibility comes into play. We are responsible for the need to acquire self-knowledge (adequate ideas about ourselves) as well as for the desire to act on them. To the extent that we remain in the sphere of self-ignorance, our actions will reflect it and we will necessarily carry the burden of responsibility for them. To the extent that we know but do not act, we carry the responsibility for our failure to act based on our true knowing. Responsibility means that we could have acted differently. We have the capability to know ourselves, since reason is our common possession, as is the ability to act on it. Reason and the ability to act on it are given to us by the necessity of our nature. To the extent that we deviate from it, we are responsible for everything we do.

This poses an interesting question: Is responsibility limited only to the area of our ignorance about ourselves, and to our actions arising from it? In other words, what is the status of responsibility with respect to free actions? The answer should by now be evident. True freedom and true responsibility are one and the same thing. A truly free act is necessarily and always a truly responsible act. There cannot be any difference between them.

3. Freedom and Responsibility: The Question of Good and Bad - Restated

We come back to the question of good and bad or good and evil. Spinoza defines good as that which we strive for (knowledge, understanding, reality, perfection, joy, happiness, pleasure). What hinders us in attaining it is considered to be evil. The same thing is described in terms of what is useful to us (good) and in terms of what we know to be harmful to us (bad). The terms useful and harmful must be construed within the context of our essence, within our endeavor to self-preserve and self-elevate (conatus). Otherwise, they could be misconstrued as plain selfishness. Selfishness is not what Spinoza meant by those terms. Our needs also include the need for association and cooperation with other human beings. This is so, since "There is nothing more useful to man than man." We can pursue our self-interest only when we can do so without injury to others. The first (self-preservation) deals with our responsibility to ourselves. The other (association and cooperation) deals with our responsibility to others. Both of these responsibilities complement and reinforce each other, they form a necessary unity.

Freedom and responsibility are synonymous when our actions are free acts. When we act on the basis of adequate ideas about ourselves and about the reality of our situation, we will necessarily act responsibly both with respect to ourselves and with respect to others. But what does to act on the basis of the reality of ourselves and of our situation mean? We come back to Spinoza's identification of reality with perfection.

4. Reality and Perfection

By reality Spinoza means what enhances our powers to act. That thing has more reality which has greater powers to produce an act. Our powers to act are to be interpreted as within the sphere of self-preservation and self-elevation. Viewed in this sense, reality is the same as perfection.

There are two aspects to reality. There is the given reality of any mode. There is also the hierarchical order of reality. Human beings occupy the highest position in this ascending order of reality within the universe of the modes. A human being has more reality than an animal, animals have more reality than plants, plants have more reality than rocks. The hierarchical order of reality rules not only vertically through the entire universe of modes but within each subsystem as well. That holds equally with respect to rocks, mountains, plants, animals and people. Thus any person can be placed in some order of reality relative to others, as well as relative to himself or herself at a different time. Our reality is not something given and fixed, but it is something changing or that can change with time. Our reality depends on our perception of it. If the perception of reality is based on adequate ideas, then our powers to act on it is greater than if it were based on delusions or hallucinations (inadequate ideas). When we improve the grasp or understanding of our reality, we simultaneously change it. In other words, we increase our powers to act on it. Hence, we gain more reality and greater perfection. To the extent that we deceive ourselves, we slide back toward less reality and less perfection.

It can thus be seen, that the perception of reality is a matter of the adequacy or truth of our ideas about it. How does this relate to the authenticity of our existence?

5. Authentic Existence

The question of authenticity of existence is related to but not identical with that of reality. Authenticity is a matter of the degree of correspondence between our beliefs (values) and our actions, as well as the degree of our self knowledge. Even if people are mistaken about themselves (their reality), they will be authentic if they sincerely strive to get to know themselves better. The process of self-knowledge is the way to the authenticity of our existence.

Each person is both a human being and a unique self. To be authentic means first and foremost to be authentically human. It means to find our true self in the context of a shared humanity. Jewish culture and tradition has recognized this aspect of our common humanity by calling such a person a *Mensch* or a human being. To call somebody a Mensch is more basic than any other designation we may assign to the person. In what follows, we delineate the existential meaning of authenticity in the context of a concretely lived life. The discussion will be held on an empirical rather than purely philosophical level. The question of the authenticity of our existence involves a series of self-clarifications. It involves getting clear and distinct ideas about ourselves. We will therefore begin with the question of unresolved inner conflict.

5.1. The Resolution of Inner Conflict

Unresolved conflicts lead to confused thinking. The confusion is primarily a confusion of ends rather than of means of attaining given ends. The more permeating and the more general the conflict, the more

176

confused will the mind be. We should distinguish betwen confusion and a lack of clarity. Lack of clarity is a normal stage in any learning process. Learning represents a movement from less clarity and less knowing to higher levels of clarity and of knowing. Confusion, especially about ends, impedes the learning process. The confused mind in its extreme manifestation is unable to think through objectively the source of its confusion.

The word "confusion" is used here differently from its use by Spinoza. Spinoza primarily has in mind confused ideas stemming from sense perception or imagination (knowledge of the first kind). Such confusion or lack of clarity is a normal part of any learning process. However, the confusion that pertains to the conflicted mind is of an entirely different order. It inhibits the mind in its ability to think clearly, dispassionately, or objectively. The confused mind tends to deny its confusion and therefore persist in it. Such confusion is more basic and more protracted. This may show itself in any activity or project. The person may fail to clarify the basic purpose of his or her intended work. The project may be too vague, too general, or insufficiently specified. It will lack concreteness. The stated objectives may be at variance with unexpressed or unconscious objectives.

5.2. Clarification of Purpose

Clarification of purpose harmonizes our existence with our goals. Clarity of purpose gives meaning to life's basic projects. This is what Spinoza did. Early in life he clarified his basic direction. He sought the path that would give him unending happiness. That path led to the knowledge of God and nature (the union of the mind with the whole of nature). This is also the advice he gives to his dearest friend when asked about the existence of a true method by which we can arrive at the knowledge of the most excellent things. After explaining the true method of knowing, Spinoza adds: "I think that in these few words I have explained and demonstrated the true method, and have at the same time, pointed out the way of acquiring it. It only remains to remind you, that all these questions demand assiduous study, and great firmness of disposition and purpose. In order to fulfill these conditions, it is of prime necessity to follow a fixed mode and plan of living, and to set before one some definite aim" (Letter 42 to I. Bresser).

The awareness of central purpose is necessary for any empirical existence. It gives us poise, harmony, balance, confidence, and most of all, a sense of direction. Without direction, things that seem connected turn out to be disjointed, and activities that seem meaningful end up lacking in meaning. The resolution of our basic direction requires the clarification of goals, aspirations, and responsibilities.

5.3. Clarification of Goals

Activities need to be defined in terms of the reason for their pursuit. Goals have to be tested with respect to the possibility of their being carried out. They have to be realistic. Realistic goals are free from self deception or wishful thinking. Considering the actuality of our existence, we are more prudent to set goals slightly under rather than over stated. In any case, we should retain a flexibility which will allow a needed modification or a reevaluation of our objectives. This raises the question of commitment to our projects.

An uncompromising and rigid commitment may freeze the person to a path and not allow him or her to alter it in light of changed circumstances or a new understanding of objective reality. The quality of a commitment pertains to the person's determination and persistence to achieve its objectives. It depends on the person's inner readiness to make it. Even here, the insistence on perfect clarity is an unrealistic supposition. We should guard against absolute notions.

Only a commitment to a highest principle can be absolute. Such commitment is not based on any *quid pro quo,* or the expectation of reciprocal rewards. "He who loves God must not require that God love him in return." Spinoza's commitment to truth was of this nature. The strength of such commitment indicates the person's strength of character. Unresolved conflicts and self-doubt will interfere with the person's ability to make and carry out his or her commitments. A weak person cannot make or or carry out a strong commitment.

5.4. Clarification of Responsibilities

A person is in the first instance responsible to himself or herself. This is the meaning of the individual's essence or *conatus.* Within this overall need to self-preserve and self-elevate, the primary responsibility is for the person to uphold his or her self respect and not to violate his or her integrity. This underlies all other responsibilities.

178

Self respect means self acceptance. It is the basis for trust in oneself and in others. To be responsible means not to assign blame to others for our shortcomings. It is a willingness and readiness to learn and to change our behavior when necessary. It is a desire to grow and to modify or overcome our character weaknesses. It means growing toward freedom.

Responsibility means awareness of the consequences of our actions both for ourselves and for others. It means to carry out our work to the best of our ability. It requires being aware of our deficiencies in meeting our responsibilities to ourselves and to others. (This will call for correction and change of any failure to live up to our responsibilities.) We need to bring into the open any irresponsible action so as to suppress any tendency to rationalize it. Only through protracted practice can we hope to change our behavior.

Often the seemingly trivial aspects of our life will reveal to us our basic tendency toward responsibility or the lack of it. For example, minor promises made but not honored, being insensitive to another person's feelings, showing a lack of consideration for someone else's circumstances, will largely indicate to us whether we practice our responsibilities or not.

When a person acts responsibly, his or her stature in the community will be enhanced. This will add to the person's inner well-being and self-respect. Our life will be enhanced when we try to simplify it and not complicate it. Simplicity means being direct without being offensive. It is being honest, aware, unafraid, and self-accepting. Life's complexities arise when we try to follow the apparent (the will of others) rather than the real (our will). The law of our existence dictates the love of ourselves. "Since reason does not demand anything contrary to one's nature, it demands that everyone loves himself, looks for what is useful.... to attain greater perfection" (EIV, 19, Schol.).

To love ourselves means to be free to experience life fully and creatively. It is to be true to our essence. Appearances complicate life, the essence simplifies it. Appearances are meant for the other, the essence is meant for ourselves.

5.5. Clarification of Aspirations

Drives and motivations take place at different levels of our consciousness, ranging from our deepest subconscious to being fully conscious. Through introspection and self-analysis we can bring our subconscious desires and aspirations into the open. We can thereby examine them with respect to their reality or objective truth. To the extent that they are based on self-knowledge and adequate ideas about ourselves, we will allow them to guide us in our actions. To the extent that they are based on delusions and self-ignorance, we will be able to rectify or suppress them.   Dreams and fantasies also have a place in our consciousness insofar as they serve as a fallback and relief from life's frustrations and insofar as they don't hold us back from our reality-oriented endeavors.

Conscious aspirations may turn into goals. To be conscious of our aspirations requires that we can recognize and read our clues. It involves sensitivity to our sensations, feelings, and signs of discomfort. Through the process of self-analysis we may free ourselves from irrational drives and substitute for these reality-tested aspirations. We act compulsively when we are driven by irrational drives. Only when such drives are confronted and dealt with consciously will they lose their inhibiting power over us. Each uncovering of irrational tendencies within us will lead to a further uncovering of such tendencies. Thus, the disclosure and bringing into the open of irrational drives become liberating agents for our conscious efforts to act freely and to move to higher levels of reality.

Irrational and exaggerated ego needs will put a strain on any relationship between two people, including marriage. The person may become dependent on his or her partner for false praise and support that feeds his or her irrational drives. This only creates a false sense of security, which makes difficult for any person to become more free. The person will be unable to formulate more realistic goals for himself or herself. A thin line separates genuine emotional support from the need to bolster the person's ego. Genuine emotional support is the single most important attribute of closeness between people. False support however (ego bolstering), will handicap rather than help the person. To know the difference between the two and to act on it, is part of life's mastery and mystery.

Excessive dependency needs originate from feelings of inadequacy. Irrational aspirations and drives may lead the person to inflict self-punishment for his or her failure to realize them. This will often turn into aggression against those who depend on the person emotionally or materially. Unconscious aspirations are in general vague and unspecified. Goals, however, must be concrete and well-defined. Such conscious goals need not exclude our hopes, dreams, or wishes. These form the essence of our desires. Such desires enrich our life regardless of circumstance or chronological age. We might stop at times and ask ourselves the simple but most often suppressed question: What do I want from life now? What are my aspirations at this point in my life? It will most likely lead to a higher spiritual awareness of ourselves.

5.6. Sense of Direction

A sense of direction reflects the internal consistency of our existence. Inner goals, aspirations, drives, and desires are integrated into the unity of the whole of our life. This integration cannot be done on the basis of reason alone. Reason has in every case to be supplemented by intuitive feeling and knowledge. The two most important decisions in our life, the choice of a marriage partner and the choice of a vocation, may serve as cases in point. Neither of these decisions can be made on reason alone. Intuitive feeling will necessarily come in into this process. But the intuition has to be founded on reason. Without it, our entire existence may go awry.

In general, to the extent that a person is true to herself or himself, a sense of direction will be inherent in the mode of her or his being. The person will appear to be focused and inner directed. He or she will not be scattered or disorganized. He or she will not get bogged down by marginal or irrelevant issues. The person will be able to differentiate and discriminate between the important and the unimportant. The need for personal questioning and self confrontation arises precisely because of a lack of clarity about our basic sense of direction. The clearer we see ourselves the less we need to face ourselves.

Yet, to know our direction and purpose in life is difficult, even under the best of circumstances. It requires vision, faith, hope, and courage. Only thus are we able to rise above the petty constraints of the present. This makes reflection and reexamination of our direction necessary. A clear sense of direction should not be confounded with outward success. Outward success is for the most part conditioned by serving the goals of others (institutions, corporations). But serving successfully the goals of others is, on principle, not different than making the self to be the purpose of our life. But we cannot make our external self (accumulation of personal trappings) the basic purpose of our life. The life of outwardly successful people may seem purposeful, yet it may really be lacking in central purpose. Nevertheless, insofar as the struggle with our sense of direction is deep and real, we can face our existence without fear. If this struggle is peripheral and superficial, it will only mask our existence in terms of our essence. It will thereby contribute to our existential anxiety. Ultimately, to have a clear sense of direction means to know ourselves and the whole of nature (God). It is the ability to view our existence *sub species aeternitatis*. It culminates in the intellectual love of God. Few people achieve this. But for life to have any meaning, we cannot really escape the need for it.

CHAPTER 11
THE BEAUTY OF SPINOZA

1. The Beauty of Spinoza's Ethics

Spinoza's *Ethics* is a profoundly powerful and beautiful text. The beauty of the *Ethics* becomes more apparent upon succesive reading. It is enhanced with understanding. When we truly understand Spinoza's *Ethics*, we cannot miss its beauty. The unrelenting identification of reality with perfection on every level of existence is connected to the beautiful. Reality like beauty, cannot be faked. Beauty is always a free affect. It cannot be forced. This is why totalitarian States lack beauty. Spinoza's quest for freedom is also a quest for beauty. It ennobles our spirit, mind, and body. The text speaks to the individual questions and problems that we all struggle with. We relate to these questions in a personal way, yet they are not only our questions, they are everybody's questions. Who of us has not grappled with questions of meaning, existence, God, truth, passions, self- knowledge, and freedom? The questions are so familiar yet the answers are so elusive. Is it ever possible to get final answers to life's questions? This is what makes Spinoza's text such a unique experience. We commune with someone who is not only among the greatest thinkers of all time, but whose character is equally unmatched and totally without blemish. Thus, we read Spinoza not only with our mind but with our heart. The beauty of Spinoza derives from an intuitive understanding of the letter and spirit imbued in the written text. Underlying this beauty is the quest for the freedom and joy of existence. Even the geometric method (*ordine geometrico demonstrata*) which initially might overwhelm and repel the reader, turns upon successive reading into an aesthetic experience. By means of the geometric method, Spinoza tells us that we are part of nature and underlie all of nature's laws and causes. Spinoza is the model of a philosopher whose search for truth is selfless and absolute. His ideas are totally free of any personal embellishment or affectation. He appeals to us in the absolute sincerity of his thoughts, and in his uncompromising pursuit of truth regardless of where it might lead. We trust his commitment to help others on their way out of existential despair, leading to more freedom, to more light, to more understanding, and to salvation.

Spinoza's argument is never forced, never dogmatic or ideological. He never pursues any hidden agenda. Whatever he wants to say, he says with utmost clarity and a minimum of words. He uses words just enough to make the exposition perfectly clear, but no more. For this, the geometric method is admirably suited. There is neither excess nor deficiency of expression in the *Ethics*. With Spinoza, reason is truly the divine gift of God to man, and he uses reason to perfection. It is the only tool that he uses, and as such it is accessible to all human beings.

God, nature or substance permeates the entire *Ethics*. The text is eternally alive, full of inner radiance and illumination. Like a beautiful painting which reveals something new every time I look at it, so it is with Spinoza's text. I can never fully exhaust its content. The clarity, simplicity and inexhaustible treasure of content evoke in the reader the free flow of reflective judgments harmonized with intuitive understanding. The latter is an unending source of great pleasure.

We find in Spinoza classical and modern constitutive elements of beauty. Plato identified the good with the beautiful, and he linked beauty to inner radiance, inner aliveness, the love of truth and the pleasures of the soul. Aristotle connected the beautiful with poetic harmony, balance, measure and temperance. For Kant, the pleasures that accompany the beautiful are derived from the free play of the imagination (creative, non-representational imagination), harmonized with the understanding. Our understanding is illuminated through the intuitive feeling of truth. Hegel's idea of beauty is the reflection of the spirit in the object. Its [beauty's] substance is contained in the spirit.[1] All of these aspects of beauty shine through in Spinoza's works. The experience of beauty, while stimulated by an outside event, object of art, or an exposure to something beautiful, is necessarily grounded in the self. It is a mode of relating and experiencing the world. It involves intuition, knowledge, the spirit and the senses. It is a mode of self- understanding, and an elevating of the person's being. It is a merging of the self with the not self and their coming together in a higher unity. This elevated unity is imbued with greater life, energy, power, and activity. The experience of beauty connects the individual to the larger whole, to nature and to the Absolute. This is what quickens our sensual and cognitive powers. The invigoration of our sensual and cognitive powers is a source of extreme pleasure. The person literally feels the transition to a higher level of reality or perfection, precisely the way Spinoza explains it.

The movement from cognitive to intuitive truth is always accompanied by a feeling of pleasure. Intuitive truth is always beautiful. It is a higher form of truth because we not only know it, but we also feel it with our body. Thus cognition is supplemented with affect. This feeling of truth with our body quickens our sensations and their mental counterparts. It revitalizes our being.

Hence the feeling of pleasure. It makes us not only want to know more, to live more, to experience more, but also to play more. That allows us to be ourselves and open ourselves up to the outside without guilt or shame. It makes us become more free, more relaxed, more self accepting, more open to play, and thereby more beautiful. The element of play and playfulness with the hermeneutics of the text allows us to get away from the aridity of conventional study and unite intellectual rigor with a joyous sensation that leads to true understanding.[2] Play frees the person from the desire to possess the object. I can enjoy things without the need to have them. By cultivating an attitude of play, I free myself from the preoccupation with myself.

This way of experiencing the world is free from any preconceived selfish desire or interest. The Kantian notion of disinterestedness as a moment in the experience of beauty comes into full play here.[3] Kant is right in saying that interest or the will to possess the object of our contemplation takes away the pleasure associated with the work of art. That deep insight into the beautiful can be generalized to hold in all of our life's endeavors. When the end result (such as, anticipated success, glory, greatness,) interferes with our activity, our activity loses its beauty and its freedom. When we are driven by our will (to shine, to excell, to be loved, admired or accepted), we lose the beauty of our work. This is true even if we are motivated in our work by a goal that is noble or idealistic, such as to make a contribution to society, to improve the social order, or to bring about greater social justice. We will still lose the beauty of our work if we are bound to it or compelled to do it by the expectation of the end result. Our work will be no more free or beautiful. It is the will that destroys the beauty. Beauty can only be present when disinterested (Kant). It is the presence of the will, whether expressed by open or suppressed desire, that makes an aesthetic experience of life so uncommon. We experience beauty only when we are free of the will for some end result. It is a most difficult problem to free ourselves from the tyranny of the will. The will is not a free cause within the person. It is usually associated with some external cause or origin. The person is mostly unaware of the true cause of his or her drive. The underlying nature of the will is in the final analysis the will to be admired or loved. This subjects the person unknowingly to a dependent status and therefore to a curtailment of the individual's freedom. It thereby destroys the beauty of people's endeavors, even if the person attains a measure of success. For the most part, however, it inhibits the very success that the will is supposed to bring about. Thus, the tyranny of the will cuts two ways: it destroys the freedom and the beauty of the act, and it destroys the pleasure as well as the free use of the person's faculties in the pursuit of the act.

This is what makes the reflection on God and nature so powerful and exhilarating. The unconditioned search for truth and reality is a free reflection. The free reflection is always joyful. It comes from the inside of the person, and is not forced on us by an outside cause. Spinoza's God is free from all will and desire. We cannot ascribe to God any human qualities. God or nature, *deus sive natura.* God or nature is all inclusive. Outside God there is nothing. God is all. There is nothing that is above or beyond nature. The supernatural does not exist. God can be rationally comprehended. God or nature has no gender, neither masculine nor feminine. While Spinoza often refers to God in the masculine pronoun, he does it only out of convention. In this, he simply follows the established tradition. "Common imagination views God as masculine, not feminine" (Letter 58 to Hugo Boxel). Nature acts with no end in view. God is a free cause and all creation is a free creation. Nature is wholly permeated with God's beauty and splendor. The experience of beauty is always a free experience. This is what makes the reflection on God so powerful and so beautiful. God is immanent in each one of us. We are free to experience God's power and beauty within us. Because God is free from will, our reflection on God is a free reflection. This free reflection is precisely our intuitive thinking and creative or artistic imagination. It is the power of God *(as Natura naturans)* acting in us. God's power of acting is mirrored in our creativity, of which genius is the extreme example.

Through our creativity, we partake in the beauty of God's creation. The perception that our mind and body are part of nature and that we are part of God's being and substance can only come about through our intuition. Through intuition we can experience the union of our mind with our body, and that this union is the same as the union of our mind with the rest of nature. Thus we can experience the immanence of God within us. This feeling and the knowledge of the whole differentiates intuition from science and from representational thinking. Representational thinking deals only with parts, since it can never encompass the whole of creation. But beauty is always connected with a grasp of the whole. This is what makes intuition a source of love, beauty, and pleasure. It is the source of all true learning and true self-understanding. It culminates in the understanding of the unity of subject and object, each one representing the inner structure of the other through their connection to the Absolute or to the whole of nature. Beauty is a progression from knowledge to intuition, from the self to the other, from the self to the not self or nature and back to the self as nature. It is a movement of the understanding that reaches its high point in the unity and harmony of the self with the whole of nature. It is the dynamic evolution of the finite understanding reaching out to grasp the infinite. Beauty is the eternal dance of the finite (as *natura naturata*) and its participation in the infinite (*natura naturans*). This recurring movement of the known and the unknown, the new and the old, and the breaking out of the new from the old (Hegel's dialectical dance and Aufhebung), is nothing but the finite trying to reach the infinite. That dynamic struggle is taking place on the level of the finite only. Here the movement is indeed dialectical. It proceeds through opposition, negation, sublation, higher levels of synthesis, and so on. All of this plays itself out around the the Absolute, whose attributes are infinite in infinite ways. Thus, all development, struggle, and progress take place in the realm of the finite, pointing to, but never reaching the Infinite. The Infinite is of necessity open ended and without limits. This means that the finite, (the human mind) can never exhaust all knowledge. Man can go toward God but can never become God. An interpretation of what Spinoza meant by the infinity of God's attributes is that while we can know the truth about God (truth is accessible to man), we can never know all the truth about God.

This reaching toward God is what Spinoza accomplishes in us. Can there be anything more powerful than that? To grasp God within me and

188

outside me? Spinoza challenges our mental powers and intensifies our quest for knowledge and self- understanding, by giving us an immeasurable wealth of ideas that are contained in his reflection on God and nature. In their absolute clarity, pristine purity and perfect economy of expression, they open themselves up to our intuitive understanding. Their inherent truth can be grasped by anyone, whatever the level of his mental grasp may be. In other words, everybody stands to gain from reading Spinoza.[4] The beauty that emanates from Spinoza's text is consistent with his definition of the beautiful. If the sensations (motions) that are communicated to us by the object (work of art) are conducive to our health, "we deem them beautiful." Beauty, Spinoza says, "is not so much a quality of the object beheld as an effect in him who beholds it"...(EI, App.).

Spinoza's works are perfectly consistent with his definition of beauty. They make us feel more knowing, more understanding, more probing, and more eager to know. If to be healthy is to be whole, they make us more whole and more healthy. They make us not only experience beauty, but become more beautiful. This is the innermost secret of beauty. The exposure to the beautiful makes the person become more beautiful.

Let us now give some examples of the power and beauty of Spinoza's ideas:

" God is the indwelling and not the transient cause of all things."

"Whatever is, is in God, and without God nothing can be or be conceived" (EI, 8 and 15).

New and old reflective associations evolve and emanate from these propositions. Whether God is transcendent or immanent, outside us or inside us, and what is the source of all truth, being, consciousness, intelligence and existence, all such questions will absorb us in our reflection on Spinoza's God. In our acquaintance with Spinoza, metaphysics has become part of our existence. That means that through Spinoza we become truly spiritualized. We rise to higher levels of being.

The two propositions reveal God's or nature's infinite power and splendor. Nothing can go against the laws of nature. They are eternal, self- caused, necessary, and free. God alone is a free cause. Everything else is conditioned to exist by God. Such divine truth can only be reached through intuition. Science can never give us a complete understanding of nature.

The beauty of divine truth rests on the combined knowing and feeling. The feeling is conditioned by the knowing. If it were the other way around, we would be experiencing ecstasy, not pleasure. Spinoza's intuitive knowing is a way of experiencing the beauty of the self and of nature. Intuitive truth is a higher form of truth than science, because it penetrates areas that science cannot reach.

The *Ethics*, one of the greatest philosophical works ever composed, is also a monument to clarity, lucidity, grace, and economy of expression. It exhibits a masterful use of language. If "love is the love of what is beautiful," as in Plato's *Symposium* and if beauty is a bridge between the individual and God,[5] than Spinoza's *Ethics* is supremely beautiful and powerful.

Let us take a few more examples from the text:

"The order and connection of ideas is the same as the order and connection of things "(EII, 7).

Spinoza's entire metaphysics is contained in this one sentence. It establishes the equivalence of all of God's attributes and of all the modes within each attribute. Each attribute equally expresses the essence of substance and each mode expresses the essence of the attribute. God is absolutely infinite, "a substance consisting in infinite attributes, of which each expresses eternal and infinite essentiality" (EI, Def.VI). Nature is represented as an interconnected system of causes, whereby the knowledge of an effect involves the knowledge of a cause, (EII, 7, Corr.). "Whatsoever exists expresses God's nature or essence in a given conditioned manner;" Each mode expresses "God's power which is the cause of all things," (EI, 36, Schol.).

In the area of human emotions, we read the following:

"An emotion can only be controlled or destroyed by another emotion contrary thereto, and with more power for controlling emotion" (EV, 7).

This proposition expresses almost all the emotional struggles of human existence. Pleasure, pain, and desire are mankind's primary emotions. All other emotions are derived from them. The ability to feel pain or pleasure is the same for all peoples, races and social strata. Contrary to St. Thomas Aquinas and the Schoolmen, emotions are not subject to control by reason. They can only be controlled by opposite emotions. This is amply evidenced in our every day existence.

Or, consider the following:

"A free man thinks of death least of all; and his wisdom is a meditation not of death but of life" (EIV, 47).

"When the mind regards itself and its power of activity, it feels pleasure" (EIII, 53).

"Self approval is in reality the highest object for which we can hope" (EIV, 52, Note).

"Desire is the actual essence of man" (EIII, Def. 1),..."it is nothing but the attempt to act" (EIV, 59 , Schol.), ... "reality... is the thing's power of action" (EIV, Preface).

"minds are not conquered by force, but by love and high mindedness" (EIV, App. 11).

"he...who is ignorant of himself, is ignorant of the foundation of all virtues..." (EIV, 56, Schol.).

"He who loves God cannot endeavor that God should love him in return" (EV, 19).

"...that we may always be determined to action by an emotion of pleasure" (EV, 10, Note).

"But all things excellent are as difficult as they are rare," concluding sentence of the *Ethics*.

The examples are meant to illustrate the beauty and the power of the text. They are not exceptional. The beauty of the *Ethics* is like that of a majestic landscape and the tenderness of a single flower. The flower and the landscape express the essence of nature. If however, we subject God (and nature) to the scrutiny of words, and if we subject the majesty and the beauty of Spinoza to the scrutiny of analytic scholarship, the beauty of God and the beauty of Spinoza will be lost.

Just like the flower loses its beauty when it is taken apart, so does intuitive truth lose its beauty when it is subjected to one-sided and narrow scholarly analysis. We remember what Spinoza said about "mere," lifeless scholarship: "my purpose is to explain, not the meaning of words, but the nature of things" (III, 20, Schol.) Spinoza is not arguing against scholarship per se. He is arguing against exaggerated and one-sided scholarship that often seeks truth in the purely linguistic analysis rather than in the nature of things. Through its complicated use of language, it often tends to obscure the truth, rather than to reveal it. This is true with respect to the higher level, open-ended, intuitive truth. Such truth cannot be scrutinized and subjected to a surgical analysis by language. This truth is too rich and too inclusive . It is therefore not susceptible to be completely contained in language. The possibilities of insight and interpretation are too numerous. This is why Spinoza should be read for the deep insights that it provides to the reader. Such insight is to be adapted to the individual's state of mind, as well as to the person's background, and culture. This means that Spinoza should be read both poetically and scholarly. Most of the Spinoza studies have taken the second road. They have primarily concentrated on the precise truth of what Spinoza meant or had to say. They have missed therefore the music, the poetry, and the beauty of Spinoza. They have missed the insight into human awareness and human nature that Spinoza stimulates and reveals. Unfortunately, narrow analytic and academic scholarship does not leave room for the grasp of the whole of life. Analytic scholarship emphasizes functionality and consistency, often at the expense of the living person. But life cannot be broken down into parts and subjected to rigid rules. Each person's life is a whole which can be only grasped intuitively. In order for the reader to benefit from Spinoza in a personal way, it is necessary to leave room for a free adaptation of Spinoza's ideas to our individual existence. It is like making it possible for us to communicate with Spinoza directly and to share with him our thoughts and problems. That is essentially what is meant by a poetic reading of Spinoza.[6] Spinoza has influenced and shaped the finest minds in the Western world. After more than a hundred years of obscurity, a time in which the Jewish ban or Cherem was remarkably effective (he was regarded as a "dead dog"), he was brought back into life and rediscovered. It happened during the Enlightenment period in late eighteenth century, in Germany.

Jacobi and Lessing, the German philsopher and German dramatist, recognized the genius of Spinoza. In their famous conversation, as quoted by Willis,[7] Lessing says: "There is no philosophy but the philosophy of Spinoza." He quotes Spinoza, who in one of his letters says "I presume not to say that I have discovered the best philosophy, but I know that I understand the philosophy that is true".[8] When Lessing asked Jacobi which direction he was going and what he is searching for, Jacobi answered: "I go towards the light of which Spinoza says that it lightens itself and darkness too, I love Spinoza."

The great German poet Goethe was a follower of Spinoza. Kuno Fischer, in his history of philosophy, calls Goethe the poet of Spinozism.[9] The noted German theologian Schleiermacher, in the midst of one of his

192

sermons, spontaneously said: "Offer with me reverently a tribute to the manes of the holy, rejected Spinoza....The high world of Spirit pervaded him; the Universe was his only and everlasting love. He was full of religion."[10] The German poet Novalis, called Spinoza "ein Gottbetrunkener Mensch" (a God intoxicated man). It was all part of the great Pantheismusstreit (the strife over pantheism) that raged in Germany, at the end of the eighteenth century. The dispute was about whether Spinoza's pantheism was to be equated with atheism. It put Spinoza at the center of the philosophical and religious thought at the time,   and his influence over   German idealism was critical and everlasting.[11]

2. The Beauty of Spinoza's Life and Character

Spinoza's life and character is an incarnation of his entire *Ethics*. As he wrote, so he lived. He achieved exactly what he set out to do ("meanwhile man conceives a human character more stable than his own, and sees that there is no reason why he should not himself acquire such a character... What that character is ...is the union existing between the mind and the rest of nature.")[12] He understood early in life that only the love and knowledge of God or nature can bring about true and enduring happiness. Spinoza sought to achieve such a character himself and "to endeavor that many should attain to it with him".[13] "All our actions and thoughts must be directed towards...one end and aim... to understand as much of nature as will enable us to attain the aforesaid character...."
Spinoza's life was "an impersonation of the grand ideal which he himself had conceived, and this was no less than ... the highest, the holiest that can be enshrined in the likeness of humanity".[14] Spinoza has been admired by the finest and most sensitive minds for his "truthfulnesss, integrity, courageousness and consistency,... for his modesty, patient and self- sufficing nature; for his gentle, conciliatory and candid disposition, for his inborn religiousness, unmixed with mysticism; for his freedom from prejudice of every kind, for his great intellectual powers, and the vast importance to the world of the works he left behind".[15] Spinoza's perfect unselfishness is what struck Goethe most, "it showed itself on every page of his writing".[16] Lucas, the first biographer of Spinoza, speaks of him with great love and admiration, although he did not fully understand his

philosophy. He tells a story about Rabbi Morteira, Spinoza's beloved teacher, who expected him to recant in order to avoid the Cherem (excommunication). However,"he was mistaken in his conjectures, for the sequel showed, that if he was well informed about the finenes of his [Spinoza's] mind, he was not well informed about its firmness." [17]

Truth, for Spinoza, was the highest principle, and his commitment to it was absolute. Freedom meant the freedom to pursue the truth, no matter where that path might lead. He cherished his freedom above everything else. He kept his needs to a modest level in order not to depend on anyone. He refused to accept monetary offers from his friends, even if these were made without any obligations, because " a man loses in his own eyes the firm and certain consciousness of an independent existence."[18] He refused a professorship at Heidelberg, because he felt that it might interfere, even minimally, with his freedom. His moral and physical courage was equally great. He was ready to confront a bloodthirsty mob, that killed the de Witt brothers (the heads of the liberal Republican party) when they were accused of treason by the political opposition.

Spinoza's character was totally without blemish. He was truly a free man and complete master of himself. The fear of death was alien to him.

The beauty of his character is transparent in his face. The Hegelian definition of beauty as the spirit reflected in the object cannot be given a better example than the transparency and the beauty of Spinoza's face and character.[19] Spinoza's life and wisdom will forever remain a shining monument to all those who value human dignity, integrity of character, and most of all , the love of truth.

Notes

1. Hans Georg Gadamer, *Truth and Method*. New York: Crossroad, 1988, p.54.
2. Ibid., pp.91-99.
3. Immanuel Kant, *Critique of Judgment*. Transl. by Werner S. Pulsar, Indianapolis: Hackett Publishing Company, Inc. 1987, p.46.
4. Gilles Deleuze, *Spinoza: Practical Philosophy*. San Francisco: City Light Books, 1988, p.1. See also, *Benedict De Spinoza Ethics*, edited

with an Introduction by James Gutmann,The Hafner Library of Classics, New York and London: Hafner Publishing Company, 1949, p.vii.

5.   Plato, *Symposium.* 206 B.

6.   Deleuze, Ibid., p.130.

7.   R. D. Willis, *Benedict de Spinoza.* London: Trubner & Co.,1870, p.153.

8.   Ibid., p.157.

9.   Ibid., p.168.

10.   Ibid., p.172.

11.   Yirmiyahu Yovel, *Spinoza and Other Heretics.* Princeton, N.J.: Princeton University Press, 1989, Vol. II, p.64.

12.   Benedict de Spinoza, *On the Improvement of the Understanding.* Transl. by R.H.M. Elwes. New York: Dover Publications, Inc. 1955, p.6.

13.   Ibid.

14.   Willis, p.1.

15.   Ibid.

16.   Ibid.,p.169.

17.   J.M. Lucas, *The Oldest Biography of Spinoza.* ed. by A. Wolf, Port Washington, N.Y./London: Kenikat Press, 1970, p.50.

18.   Kuno Fischer, *The Life and Character of Baruch Spinoza,* in William Knight, ed. *Spinoza: Four Essays,* by J.Land, Kuno Fischer, J. van Vloten, and Ernest Renan, London and Edinburgh: Williams and Norgate,1882. p.116.

19.   Arnold, Zweig, "Der Schriftsteller Spinoza" in *Spinoza Dreihundert Jahre Ewigkeit,* Spinoza Festschrift 1632-1932 by Siegfried Hessing, The Hague: Martinus Nijhoff,1962, pp.194-5. See also, Simon L. Millner, *The Face of Benedictus Spinoza.* New york: Machmadim Art Editions, Inc. 1946.

CONCLUSIONS

1.   Spinoza deconstructs the traditional view of ethics and its underlying notions of good and bad or good and evil. The religious and conventional ethics is an ethics of conduct. It is not an ethics of being. It deals with the relation of the person to the other, (the Golden rule, the Categorical Imperative). It does not deal with the relation of the person to himself or herself in freedom. However, an ethics that stresses rules of conduct rather than the person's inner freedom to pursue his or her essence (self-preservation and self-elevation) is at best superficial.   It cannot succeed in making the person truly ethical, that is, ethical from within. True morality has to be based on our inner freedom and on our clear and distinct understanding of ourselves and others. In a community of free human beings, conventional ethics becomes superfluous, since their minds are activated and joyful and their actions are freely determined from within.

Similarly, Spinoza deconstructs the traditional notions of good and bad. Good is what is useful and bad is what is harmful to the person. This has to be interpreted in the context of our essence to self-preserve and self-elevate.   What helps us to become more free, that is, to increase our powers to act in freedom and self-determination, is good. What hinders it, is bad. The scope for individual freedom for self-elevation is open-ended. It does not encroach on anybody else's freedom to pursue the same. There is no need for a conventional ethics of conduct in a society of free human beings. In conventional ethics there is an opposition between man and man. The ethics of freedom identifies the self with the other. Spinoza's Ethics is an ethics of our joyous self-determination in freedom.

2. Spinoza's philosophy has been commonly interpreted as non-teleological ("nature has no particular goal in view" (EI, App.). This needs

to be properly understood by differentiating between an assigned goal and a built-in purpose, between an initial intent and the thing's inner striving for completion. If by purpose we mean an extrinsic goal assigned to each mode by the Creator, such a purpose is ridiculed by Spinoza. If however, by purpose we understand the mode's built-in striving toward its completion, the actualization of its potentiality, then the universe is permeated with purpose. *Conatus* cannot be separated from inner purpose. Modes in nature are not conscious of their inner *telos*. Only people can be conscious of their inner purpose. Consciousness of inner purpose is necessary in order for us to become free. We cannot, however, impose a purpose on ourselves from outside ourselves. We must find our true purpose within ourselves if we are to actualize our potentiality and become "all we can be." Freedom and self direction are necessarily linked to each other. There cannot be freedom without direction, as there cannot be direction without freedom.

3. Spinoza's philosophy is the quintessential affirmation of life in joy. People actualize their essence imbued in their purpose "to be all they can be." While nature as a whole has no purpose, each mode has its inner *telos*. Only human beings can be conscious of their purpose and pursue it in freedom. Spinoza is an existentialist because his entire philosophy is anchored in existence and in life. We may regard him as the first existentialist. He is not a prophet of existential Angst, morbidity, boredom, and ennui. He is the embodiment and the joyful expression of life itself.

4. Freedom, necessity, and responsibility.
We are both free and determined. Efficient causation underlies all actions. We are variably conscious and unconscious of the true causes behind our actions. We may enlarge the scope of our freedom by becoming more conscious of ourselves and of the motivations that propel us to act in some ways. To the extent that our actions are based on reason, that is, they comply with our essence of self-preservation and self- elevation, we will act in freedom. Such actions are by necessity conscious acts. To the extent that our actions are determined by unconscious desires, that is , by passions, our actions will not comply with our essence. Thus, we act in unfreedom. Each transition from passion to reason is a transition to a higher level of reality and to freedom. Such transition is always

accompanied by a joyful feeling. The reverse is a curtailment of freedom and is accompanied by a feeling of pain.

Our essence cannot be directed against others. We cannot fulfill our essence by doing evil. This is inherent in the meaning of self-elevation. To elevate ourselves means to rise above ourselves and thus enrich and contribute to all life by our life. Therefore, when we act in freedom, we act in full responsibility, both to ourselves (self-preservation) and to others (self- elevation). Freedom pertains to choices between competing ends and the means to satisfy them. Responsibility means that we could have acted other than we actually did. A truly free act, based on adequate ideas about the self, is necessarily a responsible act. The question of responsibility cannot be distinguished from the question of freedom. Only to the extent that our actions are not free, when our actions are based on inadequate ideas about ourselves rather than self-knowledge, does the question of responsibility arise. Both the desire for self- knowledge and the desire (the affect) to act on it, to base our actions on reason, are necessary for the enlargement of the scope of our freedom. In this lies our ultimate responsibility. We are ultimately responsible for our freedom.

5. In equating freedom with self-knowledge, to act in conformance with the laws of our nature, Spinoza implores the individual to get in touch with his or her real self, with the core of his or her existential being. Only thus will we be free to fulfill ourselves and actualize our potentiality. By pointing out the right way of life, Spinoza shows us how to be true to our essence.

6. Spinoza is the philosopher of life. To understand Spinoza is to know life. This is why a purely scholarly and analytic-linguistic approach to Spinoza's works is inherently unsatisfactory and basically unrewarding. Just as we cannot dissect life (we extinguish it by doing so), we cannot splinter and dissect Spinoza. Every single thought in Spinoza is related to every other. While this accounts for the extraordinary richness and depth of Spinoza's ideas, it also contributes to its apparent difficulties and inconsistencies. Life is full of inconsistencies, and the same applies to Spinoza. He has been variously portrayed as theist and atheist, materialist and idealist, as denying freedom and upholding freedom, as denying purpose and affirming purpose. To expect Spinoza to be absolutely devoid of any discrepancies would diminish the greatness and

the   depth of his ideas. This is what makes the study of Spinoza so rewarding and enriching. We never finish it.

7.   Finally, the link between self-knowledge, self- acceptance, freedom, truth, and beauty. Only when I understand myself can I fully accept myself. Only then can I be fully relaxed with myself and therefore beautiful. My mind is active and capable to experience the free flow of creative imagination harmonized with understanding. I am open to the experience of beauty everywhere. On the other hand, when I fail to accept myself, when I remain ignorant of my true self, I am not free to be fully myself. I am therefore tense, conflicted, and not beautiful. I am unable to experience, and to see beauty even if it stares me in the face.

BIBLIOGRAPHY

Primary sources:

Original Latin:

Spinoza, Opera, ed. by J. Van Vloten and J. P. N. Land. 4 Vols. The Hague: 1914.

Gebhardt, Carl, ed. *Opera.* Heidelberg: C. Winter, 1972.

English Translations:

Britan, H. H. Transl. *The Principles of Descartes' Philosophy.* La Salle, Ill.: The Open Court Publishing Co., 1961.

Curley, Edwin, Ed. and Trans. *The Collected Works of Spinoza.* Vol. 1. Princeton, New Jersey: Princeton University Press, 1985.

Elwes, R. H. M. Transl. *The Chief Works of Benedict de Spinoza.* 2 vols. New York: Dover Publications, Inc., 1951.

Gutman, James, Ed. *Ethics, by Benedict De Spinoza.* New York and London: Hafner Publishing Company, 1949.

Shirley, Samuel, Transl. *The Ethics and Selected Letters.* Indianapolis: Hackett Publishing Company, 1982.

Runes, Dagobert D. Ed. *Baruch Spinoza: Letters to Friend and Foe.* New York: Philosophical Library, Book Sales, Inc. 1966.

Runes, Dagobert D. Ed. *Baruch Spinoza: The Road to Inner Freedom; The Ethics.* New York: Philosophical Library, Inc. 1957.

Wolf, A. Transl. *The Correspondence of Spinoza.* New york: Russell and Russell, 1966.

Wolf, A. Transl. *Short Treatise on God, Man, and His Well Being.* New York: Russell and Russell, 1967.

200

Secondary Sources and Other books

Adler, Mortimer J. *How to Think About God.* New York: Macmillan Publishing Co. Inc. 1980.

Allison, Henry E. *Benedict de Spinoza.* The Netherlands: Twayne Publishers, 1975.

Altwicker, Norbert, *Texte Zur Geschichte des Spinozismus.* Darmstadt: Wissenschaftliche Buchgesellschaft, 1971.

Ariel, David S. *The Mystic Quest: An Introduction to Jewish Mysticism..* Northvale, N.J. London: Jason Aronson, 1988.

Aristotle, *Basic Works.* Ed. by Richard McKeon, New York: Random House, 1941.

Beckett, L. C. *Neti, Neti (Not This Not that).* London: John M. Watkins, 1959.

Bennett, Jonathan, *A Study of Spinoza's Ethics.* Indianapolis: Hackett Publishing Co. 1984.

Benson, Herbert, *Beyond the Relaxation Response.* New York: The Berkley Publishing Group, 1985.

Bergson, Henri, *The Creative Mind.* New York: Greenwood Press Publishers, 1968.

Bergson Henri, *Creative Evolution.* New York: Random House, 1944.

Berrien, F. K. *Comments and Cases on Human Relations.* New York: Harper & Brothers, 1973.

Bidney, David, *The Psychology and Ethics of Spinoza.* New York: Southern Illinois University Press, 1984.

Blackman, Philip, Transl. and Ed. *Mishnayoth: Tractate Avoth.* New York: Judaica Press, Inc. 1964.

Collins, James, *Spinoza on Nature.* Carbondale and Edwardsville: Southern Illinois University Press, 1984.

Curley, E. M. *Behind the Geometrical Method.* Princeton, N. J.: Princeton University Press, 1988.

Curley, E. M. *Spinoza's Metaphysics: An Essay in Interpretation.* Cambridge, Mass.: Harvard University Press, 1969.

Curley, Edwin, and Morreau, Pierre-Francois, *Spinoza: Issues and Directions, The Proceedings of the Chicago Spinoza Conference,* Leiden, Netherlands: E. J. Brill, 1990.

De Deugd, C. *The Significance of Spinoza's First Kind of Knowledge.* Assen, Netherlands: Van Gorcum, 1966.

Deleuze, Gilles, *Spinoza: Practical Philosophy*. San Francisco: City Light Books, 1988.

Deleuze, Gilles, *Expressionism in Philosophy: Spinoza*. New York: Zone Books, 1990.

Desler Eliyahu E. *Strive for Truth!* Jerusalem: New York: Feldheim Publishers., 1978.

Donagan, Alan, *Spinoza*. Chicago: The University of Chicago Press, 1988.

Encyclopedia Judaica, Jerusalem: The Macmillan Company, 1971.

Feuer, Lewis, Samuel, *Spinoza and the Rise of Liberalism*. Boston: Beacon Press, 1958.

Freeman, E. and Mandelbaum, M. eds. *Spinoza: Essays in Interpretation*. La Salle, Ill.: Open Court, 1973.

Freud, Sigmund, *Standard Edition Of the Complete Psychological Works of Sigmund Freud*, 24 vols. Translated and edited by James Strachey, London: Hogarth Press, 1955.

Fromm, Eric, *The Art of Loving*. New York, Evanston: Harper & Row Publishers, 1956.

Fromm, Eric, *The Escape From Freedom*. New York: Avon, 1965.

Fromm, Eric, *The Heart of Man: its Genius for Good and Evil*. New York: Perennial Library, 1971.

Gadamer, Hans, Georg, *Truth and Method*. New York: Crossroad, 1988.

Gelven, Michael, *Winter, Friendship, and Guilt: The Source of Self Inquiry*. New York: Harper & Row, 1972.

Giancotti, E. Matheron, A. Walther, M. *Studia Spinozana*. Vol.1. Walther & Walther Verlag, 1985.

Greene, Marjorie, ed. *Spinoza, A Collection of Critical Essays*. Notre Dame, Indiana: University of Notre Dame Press, 1979.

Haldane, Elizabeth S. and Ross, G. R. T. *The Philosophical Works of Descartes*. 2 Vols., Cambridge: The University Press, 1970.

Hallet, H. F. *Benedict de Spinoza*. London: The Athlone Press, 1957.

Hampshire, Stuart, *Spinoza*. New York: Barnes and Noble, 1961.

Harris, Errol, E. *Salvation from Despair: A Reappraisal of Spinoza's Philosophy*. The Hague: Martinus Nijhoff, 1973.

Harris, Errol, E. *Spinoza's Philosophy: An Outline*. New Jersey, London: Humanities Press, 1992.

Hart, Alan, *Spinoza's Ethics, Part I and II, A Platonic Commentary*. Lieden: E. J. Brill, 1983.

Hegel, G. W. F. *Phenomenology of Spirit.* Oxford: Oxford University Press, 1977.

Heidegger, Martin, *Being and Time.* New York: Harper & Row Publishers. 1962.

Heschel, Abraham, Joshua, *A Passion for Truth..* New York: Ferrar Straus and Giroux, 1973.

Hessing, S. ed. *Spinoza: Dreihundert Jahre Ewigkeit.* Spinoza Festschrift, 1632-1932. The Hague: Martinus Nijhoff, 1962.

Hessing, S. ed. *Speculum Spinozanum: A Kaleidoscopic Homage, 1677-1977.* London.

Herford, Travers R. Transl. *The Ethics of the Talmud: Sayings of the Fathers.* New York: Schocken Books, 1962.

Hoffman, Edward, *The Way of Splendor, Jewish Mysticism and Modern Psychology.* Norvill, N. H. : Aronson Jason, Inc.,1981.

Hoyle, Fred, *The Nature of the Universe.* New York: The New American Library, 1955.

Hyland, Drew A. *The Virtue of Philosophy: An Interpretation of Plato's Charmides.* Athens, Ohio: Ohio University Press, 1981.

James, William. *Pragmatism.* Indianapolis: Hackett Publishing Company Co., 1981.

Joachim, H. H. *A Study of the Ethics of Spinoza.* New York: Russell and Russell, 1964.

Jowett, Benjamin, *The Dialogues of Plato.* 4 vols. Oxford: 1953.

Kak, Subhash, *The Nature of Physical Reality.* New York: Peter Lang Publishing, Inc. 1986.

Kant, Immanuel, *Critique of Judgment.* Transl. by Werner S. Pluhar, Indianapolis: Hackett Publishing Company, 1987.

Kant, Immanuel, *Prolegomena to Any Future Metaphysics,* Transl. by Lewis White Beck, New York: Macmillan Publishing Company, 1950.

Kashap, S. Paul, *Spinoza and Moral Freedom.* Albany, N. Y. : State University of New York Press, 1987.

Kierkegaard, Soren, *Concluding Unscientific Postscript.* Transl. by David F. Swenson and Walter Lowrie, Princeton: Princeton University Press, 1974.

Kline, George L. *Spinoza in Soviet Philosophy.* London: Routledge & Kegan Paul, Ltd., 1952.

Knight, William, ed. *Spinoza; Four Essays,* by T. Land, Kuno Fischer, J. Van Vloten, and Ernest Renan. London and Edinburgh: Williams and Norgate, 1882.

Kung, Hans, *Does God Exist? An Answer for Today.* New York: Wintage Books, 1981.

Leibniz, Gottfried, Wilhelm, *Discourse on Metaphysics, Correspondence with Arnauld, Monadology,* Transl. by George Montgomery, La Salle. Ill.: Open Court Pubilishing Company, 1988.

Lermond, Lucia, *The Form of Man: Human Essence in Spinoza's Ethics.* E. J. Brill, 1988.

Levin, Dan, *Spinoza: The Young Thinker Who Destroyed the Past.* New York: Weybright and Talley,1970.

Levy, Ze'ev, *Baruch or Benedict: On Some Jewish Aspects of Spinoza's Philosophy.* New York: Peter Lang Publishing,Inc. 1989.

Lukacs, Georg, History and Class Consciousness. Cambridge, Massachusetts: The MIT Press, 1971.

Mark, T. C. *Spinoza's Theory of Truth.* New York: Columbia University Press, 1972.

Martineau, James, *A Study of Spinoza.* London: Macmillan & Co. 1882.

Marx, Karl, *Capital,* Vol. 1. New York: International Publishers, 1967.

Marx, Karl, *Economic and Philosophic Manuscripts of 1844.* New York: International Publishers, 1964.

Maslow, Abraham, *Motivation and Personality.* New York: Harper & Row, 1970.

McKeon, R. P. *The Philosophy of Spinoza.* New York: Longmans, Green and Co., 1928.

Mill, J. S. and J. Bentham, *Utilitarianism and Other Essays.* edited by Alan Ryan, Harmondsworth, Middlesex, England and New York: Penguin Books, 1987.

Millner, Simon, L. *The Face of Benedictus Spinoza.* New York: Machmadim Art Editions, Inc. 1946.

Milton, Ohmer, *Alternatives to the Traditional: How Professors Teach and Students Learn.* San Francisco: Josey Bass, 1972.

Naess, Arne, *Freedom, Emotion, and Self-substance: The Structure of a Central Part of Spinoza's Ethics.* Oslo: Universitetsforlaget, 1975.

Negri, Antonio, *The Savage Anomaly: The Power of Spinoza's Metaphysics and Politics.* Minneapolis: University of Minnesota Press, 1991.

Nietzsche, F. W. *Daybreak: Thought on the Prejudices of Morality*. Cambridge: New York: Cambridge University Press, 1982.

Pagels, Heinz R. *The Cosmic Code*. Bantam Books, 1984.

Randall, John, Herman, Jr. *Aristotle*. New York: Columbia University Press, 1960.

Sartre, Jean-Paul, *Being and Nothingness*. New York: Washington Square Press, Inc. 1966.

Schelling, Friedrich, Wilhelm, Joseph von. *Of Human Freedom*. _ Chicago: Open Court Publishing Co., 1936.

Schipper, Lewis, "Innovative Teaching," in *Improving College and University Teaching*, Vol.32/Number 1, Winter 1984.

Schipper, Lewis, *A Guaranteed Employment System in the United States*. Washington, D.C.: Howard University Research Monograph No.1, 1967.

Scholem Gershom G. *Zohar: The Book of Splendor*. New York: Schocken Books, 1972.

Seielstad, George A. *Cosmic Ecology: THe View From the Outside In*. Berkeley: University of California Press, 1983.

Shaham, Robert W. and J. J. Biro, eds. *Spinoza: New Perspectives*. Norman, Okla. : University of Oklahoma, 1978.

Spinoza Symposium, *On Knowing and Being and Freedom*. Netherlands, 1973. Van Gorcum, Netherlands,1974.

Spinoza- His Thought and Work, Entretiens in Jerusalem 1977. Jerusalem: The Israel Academy of Sciences and Humanities, 1983.

St. Augustine, *Confessions*. New York: Doubleday, 1960.

Strauss, Leo, *Spinoza's Critique of Religion*. New York: Schocken Books, 1965.

Thich Nhat Hanh, *The Miracle of Mindfulness: A Manual on Meditation*. Boston: Beacon Press, 1987.

Waddington, C. H. *The Nature of Mind*. Edinburgh: Edinburgh University Press, 1972.

Wetlesen, Jon, *The Sage and the Way*. Assen: Van Gorcum, Netherlands, 1979.

Wienpahl, Paul, *The Radical Spinoza*. New York: New York University Press, 1979.

Wilbur, James, ed. *Spinoza's Metaphysics: Essays in Critical Interpretation*. Assen/Amsterdam: Van Gorcum, 1976.

Wilkins, Eliza, Gregory, *Know Thyself in Greek and Latin Literature.* New York: Garland Pub. 1979.

Willis, R. *Benedict de Spinoza.* London: Trubner & Co. , 1870.

Wolf, A. ed. *The Oldest Biography of Spinoza.* London: George Allen & Unwin Ltd.., 1927.

Wolfson, H. A. *The Philosophy of Spinoza.* 2 vols. New York: Schoken Books, 1969.

Wurzer, William S. *Nietzsche und Spinoza..* Meisenheim am Glan: Verlag Anton Hein, 1975.

Yovel, Y. *Spinoza and Other Heretics.* 2 vols. Princeton, N.J.: Princeton University Press, 1989.